Assessing
External Job Candidates

Assessing
External Job Candidates

Jean M. Phillips and Stanley M. Gully

Staffing Strategically Series

Society for Human Resource Management | Alexandria, Virginia | USA
www.shrm.org | © 2009

The Society for Human Resource Management (SHRM) is the world's largest association devoted to human resource management. Representing more than 250,000 members in over 140 countries, the Society serves the needs of HR professionals and advances the interests of the HR profession. Founded in 1948, SHRM has more than 575 affiliated chapters within the United States and subsidiary offices in China and India. Visit SHRM Online at www.shrm.org.

Library of Congress Cataloging-in-Publication Data

Phillips, Jean, 1969-
  Assessing external job candidates / Jean M. Phillips, Stanley M. Gully.
    p. cm. — (Staffing strategically series)
  Includes bibliographical references and index.
  ISBN 978-1-58644-160-9
  1. Employee selection. 2. Personnel management. 3. Employees—Recruiting. I. Gully, Stanley Morris. II. Title.
  HF5549.5.S38P489 2009
  658.3'112—dc22
                                    2009036851
10 9 8 7 6 5 4 3 2 1   09-0474

Staffing Strategically Series

ASSESSING EXTERNAL JOB CANDIDATES

ASSESSING INTERNAL JOB CANDIDATES

THE LEGAL CONTEXT OF STAFFING

STAFFING FORECASTING AND PLANNING

STAFFING TO SUPPORT BUSINESS STRATEGY

Contents

Introduction 1

External Assessment Goals 5

External Assessment Methods 19

Multiple Methods 57

Reducing Adverse Impact 59

Assessment Plans 61

Summary 65

Endnotes 67

Index 81

Acknowledgments 85

About the Authors 87

Additional SHRM-Published Books 89

Introduction

A ssessing the degree to which job candidates possess the required qualifications and characteristics to perform the job well is a critical part of staffing strategically.[1] Even if a firm's applicant pool contains some potentially great hires, if the firm's assessment system can't identify them, then they will not become employees. The goal of assessment is to identify the job candidates who would make good hires, and to screen out people who would make poor hires. A poor assessment system is little better than picking job applicants at random and giving them job offers. A well-designed assessment system can increase the number of good hires and reduce the number of bad hires an organization makes.

What difference does this make to organizations? For jobs in which there is a meaningful performance difference between high and low performers, identifying and hiring the best candidates can dramatically increase productivity and performance, and contribute directly to the company's bottom line. Consider computer programmers—the performance of star programmers can be eight to 10 times greater than the performance of average programmers.[2] In some cases, such as sales or research and development, low performers can even cost the company money. Quality candidate assessment can also enhance the performance of an organization's stock in the stock market. A survey by a large consulting firm found that a strong staffing function led to greater shareholder return. In particular, companies that had a clear idea of whom they wanted to hire and that judged applicants against clear criteria outperformed companies with weaker staffing functions.[3]

Depending on their business strategy and competitive advantage, as well as their talent philosophy and culture, different companies value different employee characteristics for similar jobs. For example, a discount retail store such as Wal-Mart that relies on low cost and high efficiency may look for efficiency-oriented candidates whom it could hire at a relatively low cost. A high-end retail store such as Tiffany's that pursues a strategy based on high-quality customer service may prefer to hire candidates who excel at customer relations and interpersonal skills, even if a higher salary is required to hire them. The choice of which candidates to hire should be based on who is likely to experience the greatest job success and who can best meet the overall hiring goals for the position, including job success, promotability, fit with the company's culture, the cost of the total rewards package, and so on.

Apache Corporation, an independent oil company, has outperformed its peers by cultivating a culture supporting fast decision-making and risk-taking. Because new hires are important in maintaining this culture, Apache looks for external candidates who have shown initiative in getting projects done at other companies.[4] The core competencies telecommunications giant AT&T considers most important to success in applicants include planning, organization, interpersonal effectiveness, decision-making, and problem analysis.[5] Yahoo! looks for really smart, passionate people who have conviction, courage, and a willingness to take some risk.[6] And Microsoft, which can receive more than 40,000 resumes a month, is only interested in hiring top talent with the skills to fulfill the core competencies of the position being filled and who have long-term potential as well.[7]

In addition to identifying the job candidates who best fit the job, the assessment system should also evaluate candidates' fit with the organization's culture and business strategy. This allows a firm to identify the job candidates best able to perform the open job and best able to help the company execute its business strategy and enhance its competitive advantage. A candidate who meets a job's technical requirements—but is also risk averse and not creative—may be a bad hire for a company pursuing an innovation strategy.

If a company wants to give employees a lot of independence and discretion, it is only by designing rigorous assessment processes that employees can later have this freedom.[8] Employees need to be selected on the basis of their work attitudes, self-leadership, and judgment to be given latitude in how they do their work. Although companies' primary hiring goal is usually job performance, some companies, including

Silicon Graphics, subscribe to the philosophy that what people know is less important than who they are. These firms believe that the primary goal of assessment is to find people with the right mind-set, attitude, and personal attributes.

Assessment methods tend to become more complex the more critical a job is to the firm and the more complex the required competencies are. If a job is difficult to do well, then it is even more important to recruit strategically, assess job candidates carefully, and choose new hires wisely.

Different assessment methods are useful for assessing different job candidate characteristics. In this book, we first discuss the different types of goals that exist for external candidate assessment, and then describe a variety of commonly used assessment methods and their strengths and weaknesses. Finally, we discuss ways of evaluating external assessment methods.

Assessing External Job Candidates is not intended as a legal reference and it does not constitute legal advice. After reading this book, you should have a good understanding of the external assessment process and how to best use different external assessment methods. Laws change and differ from state to state, and they evolve over time, so you should always consult legal counsel to ensure compliance with current local, state, and federal regulations.

External Assessment Goals

The primary goal of assessing job candidates is to identify the job candidates who will be the best hires in terms of meeting the organization's staffing goals, which usually include high job performance and enhanced business strategy execution. Identifying the job candidates who would be the worst hires is also important, as not hiring poor performers can be even more important and valuable than hiring good performers. There are a variety of other important goals organizations have when assessing external job candidates, and we discuss several of them next.

Maximizing Fit

Why are some very talented people considered undesirable hires despite their high level of skill? The answer lies in the many ways in which people need to fit with an employment opportunity to be a successful match. One goal of assessment is to maximize the degree to which the person fits the organization, workgroup, and job. We next describe each of these dimensions of fit in greater detail.[9]

Person-Job Fit

Person-job fit is the fit between a person's abilities and the demands of the job, and the fit between a person's desires and motivations and the attributes and rewards of a job.[10] Effective staffing enhances the degree to which an employee meets a job's requirements and the degree to which the job meets the individual's needs.[11] Because the most important staffing outcome is usually the new hire's job performance, person-job fit is the primary focus of most staffing efforts. From the organization's perspective, if it has an opening for an accountant, if the new hire is not an effective accountant, then the staffing effort cannot be considered successful, regardless of how many other positive staffing outcomes are achieved. In organizations that are growing rapidly, the scope of any job expands quickly. To prepare for this, Google tries to hire people who are "overqualified" for the position they are being recruited for, who can handle the expanding job duties, and who are likely to be promoted multiple times.[12]

From the applicant's perspective, if the job does not meet his or her financial, career, lifestyle, and other needs, then the match also is not ideal. An individual motivated by commissions and individually-based merit pay is not likely to be a good fit with a job based on teamwork and group rewards. Similarly, an individual who does not enjoy working with people should not be placed in a customer service position. It is not only important to consider the fit between an individual's talents and the job requirements, but also the fit between an individual's motivations and the rewards offered by the job. Research suggests that person-job fit leads to higher job performance, satisfaction, organizational commitment, and intent to stay with the company.[13]

Person-Group Fit

In addition to the fit between the recruit and the nature of the work, the fit between the recruit and his or her potential work team and supervisor is also important. Person-group fit (or person-team fit) is the match between an individual and his or her workgroup, including supervisor. Good person-group fit means that an individual fits with the goals, work styles, and skills of co-workers. Person-group fit recognizes that, in many jobs, interpersonal interactions with group members and teammates are important in getting the work done. Employees must be able to work effectively with their workgroup or teammates. Person-group fit leads to improved job satisfaction, organizational commitment, and intent to stay with the company.[14]

Because teamwork, communication, and interpersonal competencies can be as critical to team performance as team members' ability to perform core job duties, person-group fit can be particularly important when hiring for team-oriented work environments.[15] At Men's Wearhouse, CEO George Zimmer rewards team selling because shoppers want to have a positive total store experience. The company takes team selling so seriously that it even terminated one of its most successful salespeople because he focused only on his own sales figures. After firing the salesperson, the store's total sales volume increased significantly.[16] Individual characteristics such as personal goals that are consistent with those of the group, and skills that complement those of the rest of the members, are particularly important to assess in environments in which work is done in groups.

Person-Organization Fit

Person-organization fit is the fit between an individual's values, beliefs, and personality and the values, norms, and culture of the organization.[17] The strength of this fit influences important organizational outcomes including job performance, retention, job satisfaction, and organizational commitment.[18] Although it has little to no impact on meeting job requirements,[19] research has found that person-organization fit can positively influence employee attitudes and the citizenship behaviors that people exhibit beyond their job requirements, such as helping others or talking positively about the firm.[20]

Despite the potential overlap between person-job and person-organization fit, research suggests that people may experience differing degrees of fit with the job and with the organization.[21] For example, it is possible to be very good at one's job yet not feel like a good fit with the company. Conversely, it is possible to like one's employer but not be very good at one's job. Some organizational values and norms important for person-organization fit include integrity, fairness, work ethic, competitiveness, cooperativeness, and compassion for fellow employees and customers.

How can person-organization fit be maximized? One good way is to identify those applicant qualifications, competencies, and traits that relate to the organization's strategy, values, and processes. Individuals whose work styles are inconsistent with the organization's culture, business strategy, and work processes are not likely to be as successful as individuals who are good fits in these ways. For example, even if Juan is technically well qualified as a biomedical researcher, if he avoids risk, is indecisive, and tends to ruminate over a decision, he may be unsuccessful in an innovative, fast-paced, and forward-looking organization.

A new hire must be able and willing to adapt to the company by learning, negotiating, enacting, and maintaining the behaviors appropriate to the company's environment.[22] To successfully adapt, new hires must be open-minded, have sufficient information about organizational expectations and standards (and their own performance in light of those standards), and the ability to learn new behaviors and habits (e.g., low anxiety, high self-esteem, good time and stress management skills, no conflicting external obligations, etc.).

It is important to note that hiring for any type of fit does not mean hiring those whom we are most comfortable with, which can lead to dysfunctional stereotyping and discriminating against those different from ourselves who may offer a great deal to the success of the firm. One company that assesses and selects employees based on their fit with the organization and its core values is Johnson & Johnson (J&J). J&J's credo[23] clearly spells out J&J's values: customer well-being, employee well-being, community well-being, and shareholder well-being, in that order. J&J recruits, hires, and evaluates employees against its credo, which is central to J&J's organizational culture. Ralph Larsen, J&J's chairman and CEO, attributes the majority of J&J's success to its core values.[24]

In addition to having a reputation for treating employees well, Starbucks is known for its social responsibility initiatives, including outreach programs into communities both where stores operate and where its coffee is grown. Dave Pace, executive vice president for Partner Resources, Starbucks, explains, "We do it because it's the right thing to do. But from my perspective it's also a terrific recruiting and retention tool."[25] By living its values and mission statement, Starbucks is able to attract people who share its values.

Person-Vocation Fit

Person-vocation fit is the fit between a person's interests, abilities, values, and personality and his or her chosen occupation, regardless of the person's employer.[26] Worker adjustment and satisfaction are greater when their occupational environment meets their needs. For example, a social individual who dislikes detail work and working with numbers would be a poor fit with the accounting vocation.

Although individuals usually choose a vocation long before applying to an organization, understanding person-vocation fit can still be useful in staffing. Companies that would like to develop their own future leaders, or smaller organizations that need employees to fill more than one role, may be able to use applicants' vocational interests in determining whether they would be a good fit with the organization's future needs. Retaining valued employees might be easier if an organization can match their interests with a variety of career opportunities within the company. Some people pursue two or more different vocations over the course of their careers because they have diverse interests or because they become bored working in the same career for a long period. Organizations may better retain these valued career changers by understanding their vocational preferences and designing career tracks or career changes for them that place them in new roles in the organization over time that are consistent with their vocational interests and aptitudes. If successful, valued employees who would otherwise be likely to leave the organization to pursue a different type of vocation may be able to pursue multiple vocations without leaving the company.

Table 1 summarizes these four different types of fit.

Table 1. Dimensions of Fit

Type of Fit	Possible Dimensions of Fit
Person-Job Fit: the potential of an individual to meet the needs of a particular job and the potential of the job to meet the needs of the individual	Intelligence Job-related skills and competencies Job knowledge Previous experience Personality related to performing job tasks
Person-Group Fit: the match between individuals and their workgroups, including their supervisors	Teamwork skills Expertise relative to other team members Conflict management style Preference for team-based work Communication skills Personality related to working well with others
Person-Organization Fit: the fit between an individual's values, beliefs, and personality and the values, norms, and culture of the organization	Alignment between personal motivations and organizational purpose Values Goals
Person-Vocation Fit: the fit between an individual's interests, abilities, values, and personality and his or her occupation	Aptitudes Interests Personal values Long-term goals

Complementary and Supplementary Fit

There are two ways people can fit in to an organization or workgroup.[27] Complementary fit occurs when a person adds something that is missing in the organization or workgroup by being different from the others, typically by having different skills or expertise.[28] A research and development organization seeks complementary fit, for example, when it seeks scientists with new backgrounds and skills to work with existing scientists to develop a new line of products. As J.J. Allaire, founder, chairman, and executive VP of Products at Allaire Corporation, said, "It's tempting not to hire people who compensate for your weaknesses—because you don't want to admit that you have any. But … you've got to understand the strengths and weaknesses of your entire group and hire accordingly."[29]

Supplementary fit occurs when a person has characteristics that are similar to those that already exist in the organization.[30] Supplementary fit can be important when a firm needs to replace a departing customer service representative with another person who can perform the job similarly to the other customer service representatives. In this case, the organization wants to hire customer service representatives with similar skills and characteristics.

Both complementary and supplementary fit are important as together they help to ensure that new hires will fit in with the workgroup and organization but also bring new skills and perspectives that will enhance the performance of the workgroup and organization.

Assessing Accurately

Another goal of external assessment systems is that they be valid, or that they accurately identify the candidates who would be the best or worst employees. The wider the spread of talent in an applicant pool, the greater the pressure on the assessment system to weed out the bad fits and identify the good ones.

Another way to express this idea is to think about the possible outcomes of an assessment effort. Candidates can be either hired or not hired. If they are hired, then they will be either good performers or poor performers on the job. As shown in Figure 1, hiring people who become good performers generates *true positives*. Not hiring people who would have been poor performers produces *true negatives*. Both of these outcomes are desirable and are goals of the staffing effort. The two possible undesirable outcomes are not hiring people who would have been good performers, or *false negatives*, or hiring people who perform poorly, generating *false positives*. No assessment system is perfect, but more valid assessment systems do a better job than less valid ones of identifying both the most and least desirable hires from the pool of job candidates and generating high numbers of true-positive and true-negative hiring outcomes.

Figure 1. Possible Assessment Outcomes

	Poor Performer	Good Performer
Hired	False Positive	True Positive
Not Hired	True Negative	False Negative

In some jobs, one type of error can be more important than the other type. For example, false positives are particularly expensive for high-risk jobs like pilots or surgeons. False negatives, on the other hand, are particularly costly in highly competitive jobs or markets in which losing someone good to a competitor not only weakens a firm's market position but considerably strengthens its competition's. When a top scientist or salesperson chooses to join a competitor, not only does the company not acquire the top talent, its competitor is strengthened. False negatives can also be expensive when a member of a protected class is not hired, sues, and wins a big settlement.

Maximizing Return on Investment

Another important goal is maximizing the firm's return on its investment in the assessment system. Staffing should be thought of as an investment rather than a cost. The greater the return on the investment in an assessment method, the greater the assessment method's value. One assessment method may be slightly superior to another in identifying the best candidates, but if its cost exceeds the gain to the organization of hiring these slightly better candidates, then the cheaper, although less effective, method may be the better choice.

The return on investment from a new assessment method is the sum of the value of improved performance and the savings from avoiding bad hires. The value of improved performance results from subtracting the costs of using an assessment from the economic gain derived from using the assessment compared to randomly selecting candidates. The value of improved job performance resulting from using an assessment method rather than randomly selecting job candidates depends on the number of people hired, how long they stay with the company, job performance improvements resulting from using the assessment method, and the value of the performance improvements. The cost of the assessment method multiplied by the number of people assessed is the cost of using the predictor.

The value of retaining top performers should be recognized. The longer good performers stay with your company, the greater the return on the company's investment in them. Because research has shown that people who have frequently changed jobs in the past are more likely to do so in the future,[31] some companies consider frequent job changes without evidence of professional advancement as a negative factor in their hiring decision. One survey of more than 1,400 chief financial officers found that, for 87 percent of them, the length of time a job candidate has spent with previous employers was an important factor in making hiring decisions.[32] Nonetheless, because so many factors influence job tenure, we advise caution when using candidates' previous job tenure to predict their likely future job tenure.

Generating Positive Stakeholder Reactions

Meeting the needs of different stakeholders in the staffing process is another assessment goal. Recruits, hiring managers, and recruiters should all be satisfied with the processes and outcomes involved in using an assessment method. For example, requiring hiring managers to take three hours out of their busy day to interview each job candidate may meet with resistance, and may not even be possible. Recruiters may feel that doing 20-minute phone interviews to prescreen each job applicant is too burdensome, and applicants may feel that three separate visits for different assessments are excessive. Although an assessment method may be valid and identify the best and worst job candidates, if it does not also meet the needs of the stakeholders using them (and the stakeholders whom it assesses), then it is not as effective as it could be.

An assessment method's speed, usability, and ability to predict job success all influence the ease of getting people in the organization to use it correctly and consistently. Training recruiters and hiring managers in the use of the technique and its benefits, assessing and rewarding them for using it correctly and consistently, and having an assessment system expert available to help when needed can increase the correct and consistent use of new assessment methods.

Supporting the Firm's Business Strategy, Talent Philosophy, and HR Strategy

Strategic staffing supports and enables business strategy execution. McDonald's is a good example. Its business strategy relies on providing customers quality, cleanliness, quick service, and value, and the company works hard at hiring people who want to excel in delivering outstanding service. It tries to recruit and hire the best people, retain them by offering ongoing training relevant to their position,[33] and promote from within to fill management positions.[34]

Another goal of an assessment system is to support the organization's talent philosophy and HR strategy. Viewing applicants and employees as investors might stimulate a company to incorporate more interviews into the assessment process and develop a comprehensive careers section on its web site to allow candidates ample opportunity to learn as much as possible about the company before joining. A firm viewing employees as assets may focus on efficient candidate assessment and minimize candidates' opportunities to meet with a variety of organizational representatives to learn about potential co-workers and supervisors. An organization that wants people to contribute over long-term careers should evaluate job candidates in terms of their long-term career potential within the company, rather than evaluate them just for the current open position. In this case, identifying the competencies, styles, and traits required for career advancement within the company is also relevant. If an organization does not plan to promote from within, its recruitment profile and screening criteria should focus only on the open position.

Establishing and Reinforcing the Firm's Employer Image

Another goal of external assessment can be to establish and maintain an organization's employer image. A company that wants to be perceived as an innovative and engaging place to work might reinforce that image during the assessment process by asking applicants challenging interview questions that require creativity. Every interaction job applicants have with a firm establishes and reinforces the firm's employer image, and one of the goals of the assessment process should be to consistently reinforce the firm's desired image.

Identifying Development Needs

Assessment tests can also identify new hires' developmental needs. If a top candidate's assessment scores shows that his organization and time management skills are good but his customer service skills need further development, post-hire training can improve these skills. Some assessment methods even identify applicants' preferred learning style, which can decrease training time, improve training effectiveness, and increase retention.[35]

Assessing Ethically

Ethics is an important issue in staffing, particularly in assessment. The entire selection process needs to be managed ethically, including honestly explaining how test results will be used and how candidates' privacy will be protected, and communicating with candidates when promised. Firms need to think through the ethics of using assessment methods applicants find invasive, including integrity tests and genetic tests. The people administering an assessment need to be properly trained and appropriately qualified, and applicants' privacy needs to be protected at all times.

Complying with the Law

Legal issues loom large when it comes to assessment, and companies have good reason to protect themselves against potential charges of hiring discrimination. In addition to the negative publicity generated by a lawsuit, plaintiffs are often successful and court awards regularly run into the hundreds of thousands of dollars. One landmark case in this area is *Griggs v. Duke Power Company*.[36] In this case, the Supreme Court found that under Title VII of the Civil Rights Act of 1964, if an employment test disparately impacts ethnic minority groups, the firm must demonstrate that the test is "reasonably related" to the job for which the test is required. Credit checks, background checks, and cognitive ability tests are among the most likely assessment methods to result in disparate impact.

Following the Uniform Guidelines on Employee Selection Procedures,[37] which were created to provide employers guidance in complying with the law, and conducting fair, consistent, and objective assessments are important to legal compliance. We discuss these next.

Uniform Guidelines on Employee Selection Procedures

In 1978, the need for a consistent set of principles on the use of tests and other assessment and selection procedures prompted The Equal Employment Opportunity Commission (EEOC), the Civil Service Commission, the Department of Labor, and the Department of Justice to jointly adopt the Uniform Guidelines on Employee Selection Procedures (UGESP). The UGESP assist organizations in complying with requirements of federal law prohibiting race, color, religion, sex, and national origin discrimination in hiring practices by providing a framework for determining the proper use of tests and other assessment procedures. Under Title VII, the UGESP apply to the federal government with regard to federal employment, to most private employers with at least 15 employees for 20 weeks or more a calendar year, to most labor organizations, apprenticeship committees, and employment agencies, and to state and local governments with at least 15 employees. Through Executive Order 11246, they also apply to federal government contractors and subcontractors.[38]

Here are some sample guidelines:[39]

- A test of knowledge and abilities may be used if it measures a representative sample of knowledge, skills or abilities that are necessary to performance of the job and are operationally defined.

- Knowledges must be defined in terms of behavior, and each knowledge must be part of a body of learned information that is actually used in and necessary for required, observable job behaviors.

- Abilities must be defined in terms of observable aspects of job behavior and each ability should be necessary for the performance of important work behaviors. Any selection procedure measuring an ability should closely approximate an observable work behavior.

- To the extent that the setting and manner of the administration of the selection procedure fails to resemble the work situation, the less likely it is that the selection procedure is content valid, and the greater the need for other validity evidence.

The entire UGESP are available online,[40] and staffing specialists should develop a thorough knowledge of them. *The Principles for the Validation and Use of Personnel Selection Procedures*[41] and the *Standards for Educational and Psychological Testing*[42] are also important documents that provide standards and guidelines for developing and using various assessment methods.

Fair, Consistent, and Objective Assessments

Good hiring practices compare all applicants using the same fair, consistent, and objective information predictive of job success. A false or contradictory reason given for not hiring someone can be considered an excuse for discrimination. For example, if an employer states that an applicant was not hired because of insufficient experience, but the successful candidate has less experience, the contradiction can be interpreted as a pretext for discrimination.

One employment law expert advises companies to drop the use of vague terms such as "best fit" when documenting why someone was hired because the ambiguity makes it more difficult to reconstruct the selection process and explain why the candidate was chosen.[43] Recruiters and hiring managers should be able to articulate objective, neutral reasons for rejecting or hiring any applicant. The required qualifications must make sense to the EEOC and its state-level equivalents who are looking for a simple, fair process that treats all applicants the same.

Consistently applied, objective assessment methods based on bona fide occupational qualifications derived from a job analysis are best for legal compliance. Subjective assessment criteria that involve speculation about customer preferences or how a candidate is likely to perform on the job are not advisable. Although it is not illegal to reject someone based on subjective evaluations and speculation, subjective evaluations and speculation are precursors to stereotyping, and rejecting candidates based on stereotypes can quickly get employers into legal trouble.[44]

External Assessment Methods

Typically, job candidate assessment is done in waves. When people first apply for a job, they are *job applicants* and are evaluated against the minimum acceptable criteria for the job, such as relevant education and skills. The purpose of these screening assessment methods is to narrow the pool of job applicants to a smaller group of *job candidates.* Job candidates are then assessed in more depth using evaluative assessment methods that evaluate the pool of job candidates to determine whom to hire. Job offers may be made contingent on passing contingent assessment methods. Contingent assessments are used when the firm has identified whom it wants to hire, and if the finalist passes the contingent assessment (typically a background check, drug screen, etc.), he or she receives a formal job offer. Assessments tend to get more detailed and rigorous as people move from being job applicants to job-offer receivers.

Table 2 summarizes the general effectiveness of the assessment methods we discuss next in predicting job performance (validity), applicant reactions, relative cost compared to other assessment methods, adverse impact, and ease of use. Validity ranges from -1 to +1, and reflects the strength of the relationship between the assessment and job performance. Validities closer to -1 and +1 reflect better prediction of job performance than do values closer to 0. A validity of 0 would reflect no relationship between the assessment and job performance, meaning that that particular assessment is useless in predicting performance for the job being studied. The values presented are typical of those found in organizations, but the exact validity, cost, and adverse impact will vary from job to job and from company to company. In most circumstances, we rarely see validities remotely approaching +1 or -1. Even the relationship between people's height and weight is typically less than 0.80. Because we rarely have such precisely measured and highly correlated data, the typical values we might see in staffing contexts are between +0.40 and –0.40. Although much lower than the theoretical maximum and minimum, these values can result in significant improvements in the quality of hires.

We advise particular caution in the case of validity, as the values presented are averages and may vary considerably depending on the job and organization. The table is useful as a general guide, but companies should always check for themselves how useful any predictor is in their context. Differences in the quality of an assessment method's development, the degree of training users receive, and how consistently the tools are used can all influence the costs and validity of any assessment method as well as its adverse impact and applicant reactions to it.

When choosing which assessment methods to use, it is important to match the assessment method to the characteristic or competency of interest, and to consider the other assessment methods that will be used. In some cases, cognitive ability tests may predict job performance beyond structured interviews, and in other cases, the two might be found to overlap considerably, in which case using only one of the two can save time and money. Because no assessment method is perfect, it is best to use multiple methods when assessing applicants. We next discuss a variety of commonly used assessment methods and how they are best used.

Although we group the following external assessment methods into screening, evaluative, and contingent categories based on how they are typically used, it is possible to use any screening or evaluative assessment method at any time during the hiring process. Contingent assessment methods must be administered after a contingent job offer is extended.

Screening Assessment Methods

Resumes and Cover Letters
Although little research exists on the validity or adverse impact of using resumes as an assessment method, resumes and cover letters have historically been a core part of the hiring process. Applicants volunteer information about themselves and their interest in the position in a cover letter, and provide a resume summarizing their relevant education and work and nonwork experiences. Technology has facilitated the management of the large number of resumes companies often receive,

Table 2. Comparison of Some Commonly Used External Assessment Methods

Assessment Method	Average Validity[a]*	Applicant Reactions[b]	Relative Costs[c] (Development/ Administration)	Adverse Impact	Usability
Assessment centers	0.37	Good	High/high	Low	Difficult
Cognitive ability tests	0.51	OK	Low/low	High	Easy
Integrity tests	0.41	OK	Low/low	Low	Easy
Job knowledge tests	0.48	OK	High/low	Low	Easy
Reference checks	0.26	OK	Low/low	Low	Easy
Situational judgment tests	0.34	Good	High/low	Low	Moderate
Structured interviews	0.51-0.63	Good	High/high	Mixed	Moderate
Unstructured interviews	0.20-0.38	OK	Low/high	Mixed	Easy
Personality testing	-0.13-0.33 (Depends on the trait)	OK	High/low	Low	Easy
Biodata	0.35	OK	High/low	Low	Easy
Weighted application forms	0.50	Good	High/low	Low	Easy
Simulations	0.54	Good	High/high	Low	Difficult
Work samples	0.33	Good	High/high	Low	Difficult

*Validity values range from -1 to 1, with numbers closer to -1 or +1 reflecting better prediction of job performance.

[a] Source for validity coefficients: Schmidt, F.L. & Hunter, J.E. (1998). "The validity and utility of selection methods in personnel psychology: Practical and theoretical implications of 85 years of research findings," *Psychological Bulletin*, 124, 262-74; Situational judgment test validity is from McDaniel, M.A., Morgeson, F.P., Finnegan, E.B., Campion, M.A., & Braverman, E.P. (2001). Use of situational judgment tests to predict job performance: A clarification of the literature. *Journal of Applied Psychology*, 86, 730-40; Biodata validity is from Reilly, R.R. and Chao, G.T., "Validity and Fairness of Some Alternative Employee Selection Procedures," *Personnel Psychology*, 1982, 35, 1-62; work sample validity is from Roth, P.L., Bobko, P., McFarland, L.A., "A Meta-analytic Analysis of Work Sample Test Validity: Updating and Integrating Some Classic Literature," *Personnel Psychology*, 2005, 58 (4), 1009–37; for structured and unstructured interviews also from McDaniel, M.A., Whetzel, D.L., Schmidt, F.L., & Maurer, S.D., "The Validity of Employment Interviews: A Comprehensive Review and Meta-Analysis," *Journal of Applied Psychology*, 1994, 79 (4), 599-616 and Weisner, W.H. & Cronshaw, S.F., "A Meta-analytic Investigation of the Impact of Interview Format and Degree of Structure on the Validity of the Employment Interview," *Journal of Occupational Psychology*, 1988, 61, 275-90.

[b] Based in part on Hausknecht, J.P., Day, D.V., & Thomas, S.C., "Applicant Reactions to Selection Procedures: An Updated Model and Meta-Analysis," *Personnel Psychology*, 2004, 57(3), pp. 639-683; Coyne, I. & Bartram, D., "Assessing the Effectiveness of Integrity Tests: A Review," *International Journal of Testing*, 2002, 2 (1), 15-34.

[c] From Ryan, A.M. & Tippins, N.T., "Attracting and Selecting: What Psychological Research Tells Us," *Human Resource Management*, 2004, 43, pp. 305–18.

and scanners and software tools have made it possible for firms to do a better job searching them for relevant information. One of the biggest drawbacks of resumes and cover letters is that applicants do not use the same format or include the same information in their resumes, which can make it difficult to compare them.

Because the information put on resumes may not be accurate, it is important to confirm the accuracy of any resume information in making screening decisions. Experts estimate that 10 percent to 30 percent of job seekers shade the truth or flat-out lie on their resumes, particularly in the areas of education, previous compensation, reason for leaving, and previous job titles and accomplishments.[45] The fact that firms have even fired CEOs after discovering that they have inflated their educational credentials illustrates how important it is to confirm the accuracy of all self-reported information used to make hiring decisions.[46] False information can be reduced by requiring applicants to sign a statement

---

Table 3. Actual Resume Blunders

These are from actual resumes:[a]

- "You are privileged to receive my resume."
- "Able to say the ABCs backward in under five seconds."
- "I often use a laptap."
- "I will accept nothing less than $18 annually."
- "I am very detail-oreinted."
- Reason for leaving last job: "Pushed aside so the vice president's girlfriend could steal my job."
- Accomplishments: "Completed 11 years of high school."
- "I am relatively intelligent, obedient, and as loyal as a puppy."
- Specified that his availability to work Fridays, Saturdays, or Sundays "is limited because the weekends are 'drinking time.' "
- Explained a three-month gap in employment by saying that he was getting over the death of his cat.
- Explained an arrest record by stating, "We stole a pig, but it was a really small pig."

[a] Fisher, A., "10 Dumbest Resume Blunders," *Fortune*, April 25, 2007, available online at: http://money.cnn.com/2007/04/25/news/economy/resume.blunders.fortune/index.htm?postversion=2007042510. Accessed February 4, 2009; "Resume Quotations," Offshore-environment.com, 2007, available online at: http://www.offshore-environment.com/takebreak.html. Accessed February 4, 2009; Robert Half International, "Real-Life Blunders to Avoid," Yahoo! Hotjobs, 2007, available online at: http://hotjobs.yahoo.com/jobseeker/tools/ept/careerArticlesPost.html?post=57. Accessed February 4, 2009.

when submitting an application or resume that knowingly falsifying this information can result in immediate termination.

Because many firms now use automated resume scanning and screening software, it is important to proofread your own resume and cover letter for accuracy and to correct any typographical or spelling errors. If a word the firm uses to screen candidates is misspelled, the computer system won't identify your resume as a good match. Just for fun, Table 3 contained some actual resume and cover letter blunders.

Job Applications

Job applications require applicants to provide written information about their skills and education, job experiences, and other job-relevant information. Although the information on an application may replicate information already contained on a resume, applications help to ensure that consistent information is collected from each applicant and help to check the accuracy of the information provided. Although job applications often contain a statement that providing inaccurate information is grounds for dismissal, it is still best to verify any information used to screen candidates. Figure 2 shows a typical job application form.

To standardize the information collected from job applicants, some organizations have begun using online applications. When job seekers apply at any of The Fresh Market gourmet grocer locations, they first complete an online employment application. Within minutes of finishing the less than 30-minute application, the hiring manager receives a three-page report via e-mail that summarizes the biographical information provided by the individual, answers to the application and an analysis of the answers, and a page of follow-up interview questions if the applicant passes the screening.[47]

To take the subjectivity out of the store manager's interview process, McDonald's developed an online application for job candidates in the United States that asks candidates questions about their work experiences, preferences, and how they would respond to certain situations. Based on the results, the questionnaire prompts a green light to the hiring manager, signaling that the candidate would be a good hire; a yellow light, meaning that the manager should ask more questions; or a red light, meaning do not hire the person.[48]

Figure 2. Job Application Form

Many employers require all applicants, regardless of the job they apply for, to complete a job application form. This way the employer will have consistent data on file for all prospective applicants. Individual state and federal laws should always be reviewed prior to developing an application.

Instructions: Print clearly in black or blue ink. Answer all questions. Sign and date the form.

Position Applied For: _____ Today's Date: _____

PERSONAL INFORMATION

Full Name _____

Street Address _____

City, State, Zip Code _____

Phone Number (_____)_____

Are you eligible to work in the United States?   Yes ☐   No ☐

If you are under age 18, do you have an employment/age certificates?   Yes ☐   No ☐

Have you been convicted of or pleaded no contest to a felony within

the last five years?   Yes ☐   No ☐

If yes, please explain: _____

_____

AVAILABILITY

Days/Hours Available: Monday from _____ to _____

Tuesday from _____ to _____

Wednesday from _____ to _____

Thursday from _____ to _____

Friday from _____ to _____

Saturday from_____ to _____

Sunday from _____ to _____

What date are you available to start work? _____

EDUCATION

Name and Address of School Degree/Diploma Graduation Date

_____

_____

_____

_____

Job Application Form continued on next page

Figure 2. Job Application Form continued

Skills and Qualifications: Licenses, Skills, Training, Awards

_____

_____

_____

EMPLOYMENT HISTORY

Present or Last Position: _____

_____

Employer:_____

Address: _____

Supervisor:_____

Phone:_____

E-mail:_____

Position Title: _____

From: _____ to: _____

Responsibilities: _____

_____

Salary: _____

Reason for Leaving: _____

May We Contact This Employer?   Yes ☐   No ☐

THREE REFERENCES (required)

Name/Title Address Phone

_____

_____

_____

I certify that information contained in this application is true and complete.

I understand that providing false information may be grounds for not hiring me or for immediate termination of employment at any point in the future, if I am hired. I authorize the verification of any or all information listed above.

Signature _____ Date _____

Online applications can not only be fast and cost-efficient, they can greatly reduce the initial assessment burden placed on recruiters or hiring managers. Using web-based assessment tools for screening applicants applying for hourly positions decreased the number of employment interviews Sherwin-Williams conducts each year by more than 5,000. The higher quality hires made after implementing an online candidate assessment system also reduced turnover among hourly workers at Kroger grocery stores by 25 percent, meaning that the company now spends 25 percent less time recruiting and hiring candidates.[49]

In addition to providing in-store kiosks at which online applications can be completed, employers, including American Express, now direct job seekers to their corporate web site to answer a series of preliminary screening questions (e.g., degrees obtained, willingness to relocate, etc.) and apply for jobs. American Express uses its questionnaire to weed out the bottom half of candidates and allow recruiters to focus their time and attention on more promising applicants.[50]

Weighted Application Blanks

The information collected on a job application can be weighted according to its importance. The relative importance and relative time spent on assessments made for each job duty during the job analysis can inform these weights.[51] The degree to which different blank information on applications differentiates high- and low-performers can also inform the weights to use for each item. When information receives different weights, the assessment method is a weighted application blank. As shown previously in Table 2, weighted application blanks are received well by applicants, relatively inexpensive, easy to use, and have an average validity of 0.50.

Developing a weighted application blank involves:
1. Selecting an employee characteristic to be measured (job performance, tenure, etc.);
2. Identifying which job application questions predict the desired employee behaviors and outcomes;
3. Evaluating the questions' relative predictive power;
4. Assigning weighted values to each relevant question; and
5. Scoring each applicant's completed job application form using the scoring key.

Candidate advancement decisions are made according to applicants' weighted scores. It can even be possible to determine, for a given job application form, the total score below which a prospective employee might be a bad risk for the company and above which the applicant is likely to be a successful employee.[52] Weighted application blanks look like regular application blanks, and applicants typically do not know that a weighted scoring system will be used to evaluate their answers. Although this encourages honest answers, any applicant-provided information should be verified if it is to be used in making a hiring decision. Figure 3 shows a sample (fictitious) weighted application blank scoring key for a sales associate position.

Figure 3. Weighted Application Blank Scoring Key for a Sales Associate Position

Previous Occupation Social +1 Not social -1	*Full- or Part-Time Preference* Full time +2 Part time -1
Education 8 years 0 9-10 years +1 11-12 years +2 12-13 years +3 Over 13 years +2	*Confidence* Replies to question, "What amount are you confident of selling each month" +1 Does not reply to question -1
Personal Sales Experience Previous sales experience +2	*Family Sales Industry* Has anyone in family ever worked in sales? Yes +2 No 0

One criticism of the weighted application blank is that it doesn't matter why an item differentiates successful from unsuccessful performers, only that it does. To maximize the chances that an item will work over time, it is best to know or at least have an idea why the question predicts job success. For example, asking whether someone was ever captain of a sports team is a clear indicator of leadership. Weighted application blanks have been used successfully with production workers,[53] scientists,[54] and life insurance salespeople.[55]

Biographical Information (Biodata)

Biographical information, also referred to as biodata, is collected through questions about candidates' interests, work experiences, training, and education, assessing a variety of personal characteristics such as achievement orientation and preferences for group vs. individual work. Biodata permit "the respondent to describe himself in terms of demographic, experimental, or attitudinal variables presumed or demonstrated to be related to personality structure, personal adjustment, or success in social, educational, or occupational pursuits."[56] Biodata can be collected as part of a job application or via a separate questionnaire.

Biodata, when properly done, is both highly valid[57] and generally low in adverse impact,[58] although faking, invasion of privacy, and adverse impact are possible issues. Adverse impact may depend on the degree to which items directly or indirectly reflect cultural differences in social, educational, or economic advancement opportunities. Thus, in constructing inventories, include items with the potential for reducing adverse impact, and validate and check the biodata for adverse impact before using it in making hiring decisions. Very little information exists to support or refute allegations of inaccuracy, invasion of privacy, or faking.[59] Guidelines, regulations, and statutes restrict certain types of information from being included on biodata inventories to protect applicants from being denied employment based on factors unrelated to jobs. Unless demonstrated to be job-relevant, items addressing race, gender, marital status, number of dependents, birth order, and spouse's occupation are not appropriate as a basis for selection decisions. As long as they are correlated with job success or related to "business necessity," other personal items such as grade point average or level of education can be used for personnel decisions, although their tendency to cause adverse impact needs to be checked. Table 4 contains some sample biodata items.

For moral, ethical, and legal reasons, biodata items should not be intrusive or make the respondent uncomfortable. In general, a biodata item should not inquire about activities to which not everyone has equal access, or about events over which the individual has no control.[60] Nonetheless, just because one respondent was a captain on a sports team and another respondent went to a small school without sports teams does

Table 4. Sample Biodata Items

Choose the best response to each question.

1. How many different paying jobs have you held for more than 2 weeks in the past year?
a.   5-6
b.   3-4
c.   1-2
d.   None

2. In my leisure time, the activities I most enjoy doing are:
a.   Team sports
b.   Individual sports
c.   Constructing things
d.   Reading
e.   Social activities
f.   None of the above

3. Have any of your family ever worked in this industry?   Yes ☐   No ☐

4 Have you ever repaired small motors at home?   Yes ☐   No ☐

not diminish the first respondent's accomplishments. This highlights the balance we must strike when using biodata items.[61]

As shown in Table 2, well-developed biodata items can have moderate predictive validity (average validity of 0.35) for a variety of criteria including training, job performance, tenure, and promotions.[62] When properly done, biodata is also among the best assessment techniques in terms of minimizing adverse impact, although applicants tend to perceive them as invasive[63] and different keys may be needed for males and females.[64] Biodata have been used to predict many aspects of job success with many different jobs, including research competence and creativity.[65]

Creating a biodata assessment to improve job performance involves:

1. Defining job performance;
2. Identifying highly successful employees;
3. Collecting biographical data;
4. Correlating biographical data with the performance scores;
5. Creating the final biodata form; and
6. Testing, using, and continually checking the accuracy of the biodata.

An example of a biodata formula predicting secretary tenure that would be derived from biodata collected from real secretaries is:

Tenure = (3.1 * years of education)
+ (4.2 * years of related job experience)
− (1.4 * miles from office)

Biodata has been used successfully to predict success with electricians,[66] blue-collar workers,[67] and managers.[68] Internet search company Google asks job applicants to complete an elaborate online survey that explores their attitudes, behavior, personality, and biographical details going back to high school. The questions range from the age when applicants first got excited about computers to whether they have ever tutored or established a nonprofit organization and are used to predict how well a person will fit into Google's culture. To create the biodata formulas, Google asked every employee who had been working at the company for at least five months to fill out a 300-question survey. It then compared this data with 25 separate measures of each employee's performance, including the employee's supervisor and peer performance reviews, and their compensation to identify which biodata items predicted performance.[69]

The difference between job applications, weighted application blanks, and biodata can be confusing. Job applications are the forms job applicants expect to complete to provide information about themselves when they are applying for a job. Weighted application blanks look like regular job application forms, but unlike regular job applications, applicant responses are scored and combined to determine the individual's likely fit with the job and organization. Biodata is the personal information that predicts aspects of job success. Job applications may contain biodata items, but do not have to. Weighted application blanks are designed to assess different types of biodata. When items on a job application are evaluated to determine how well they predict job success, these items become biodata. For example, asking applicants to state their years of experience in the industry could be a minimum qualifications question on a job application, but when people's responses to that question are correlated with subsequent job performance, then it becomes biodata. Biodata can also be assessed via a separate questionnaire. As with any assessment, job applications, weighted application blanks, and biodata should not be used alone. They should be a part of a system that uses several types of assessments to evaluate different aspects of likely job performance. Job applications, weighted application blanks, and biodata are most commonly used early on in the hiring process as screening assessment methods.

Telephone Screens

Many firms use quick telephone screens to assess applicants' availability, interest, and preliminary qualifications for a job. Some recruiters use the phone interview to assess a job's fit with the applicant's noncompensatory screening factors to prevent both parties from wasting time. Other recruiters use the telephone screen as a way to develop a more thorough picture of the individual and/or to give him or her a good impression of the company. The phone screen can also help to identify other positions with which the applicant might be a good fit.[70]

One common assessment mistake companies make is to assume that highly qualified and experienced applicants wouldn't be happy in a job with less responsibility than positions they've held in the past. This assumption can be incorrect, as there are many reasons people may want to move to lower-stress and lower-responsibility positions, including the opportunity to work for a stable and growing company, a positive work environment, and the challenge of learning new things. Highly qualified people are likely to get up-to-speed faster (saving training costs), help mentor other employees, and can be a good value. A quick telephone screen can allow a seemingly overqualified applicant to elaborate on his or her interest in the position and receptiveness to accepting a lower salary.[71]

Evaluative Assessment Methods

Cognitive Ability Tests

Individuals with higher levels of general mental ability acquire new information more easily and more quickly, and are able to use that information more effectively. Frank Schmidt and Jack Hunter's[72] research suggests that general cognitive ability influences job performance largely through its role in the acquisition and use of information about how to do one's job. Research has supported the idea that cognitive ability is more important in complex jobs, when individuals are new to the job, and when there are changes in the workplace that require workers to learn new ways of performing their jobs.[73] Some companies, including Internet search firm Google, prefer to hire for intelligence rather than experience.[74]

Cognitive ability tests typically use computerized or paper-and-pencil tests to assess candidates' general mental abilities, including verbal or mathematical reasoning, logic, and perceptual abilities. Because scores on these tests can predict a person's ability to learn in training or on the job,[75] be adaptable and solve problems, and tolerate routine, their predictive value may increase given the trend toward jobs requiring innovation, continual training, and nonroutine problem-solving. There are many different types of cognitive ability tests, including the Wonderlic Personnel Test, Raven's Progressive Matrices, the Kaufman Brief Intelligence Test, and the Wechsler Abbreviated Scale of Intelligence. Table 5 contains some questions similar to those found on the Wonderlic Personnel Test.

Table 5. Cognitive Ability Test Items

The following questions are like those found on the Wonderlic Personnel Test measuring cognitive ability. The answers are at the bottom of the table.

1. Assume the first 2 statements are true. Is the final one: 1. True 2. False 3. Not certain
   - The boy plays baseball.
   - All baseball players wear hats.
   - The boy wears a hat.

2. Paper sells for 21 cents per pad. What will 4 pads cost?

3. How many of the five pairs of items listed below are exact duplicates?

Nieman, K.M.	Neiman, K.M.
Thomas, G.K.	Thomas, C.K.
Hoff, J.P.	Hoff, J.P.
Pino, L.R.	Pina, L.R.
Warner, T.S.	Wanner, T.S.

4. RESENT RESERVE—Do these words
   a. Have similar meanings?
   b. Have contradictory meanings?
   c. Mean neither the same nor opposite?

Answers: 1) True 2) 84¢ 3) 1 4) c

Despite being easy to use and one of the most valid selection methods for all jobs, with an average validity of 0.51, cognitive ability tests produce racial differences that are three to five times larger than other predictors, such as biodata, personality inventories, and structured interviews, that are also valid predictors of job performance.[76] Although the reasons for the disparate impact are not fully understood, it is thought that factors including culture, differential access to test coaching and test preparation programs, and different test motivation levels due to different perceptions of the test's validity among people in different subgroups.[77] Applicants also often dislike cognitive ability tests because they don't seem job-related.[78]

Because disparate impact can be problematic when using cognitive ability tests,[79] employers should evaluate the effect of cognitive ability tests on protected groups before using them on their own job candidates. Because cognitive ability tests can often be combined with other predictors such that adverse impact is reduced while overall validity is increased, and because alternative predictors with less adverse impact can produce validity coefficients comparable to those obtained with cognitive ability tests alone, cognitive ability tests should generally not be used alone.[80] We stress that no assessment method is best used alone, but this is particularly true in the case of cognitive ability tests. Many organizations use cognitive ability tests, including the National Football League.[81]

Noncognitive Ability Tests

Tests can also measure psychomotor, sensory, and physical abilities. Psychomotor tests assess a person's capacity to manipulate and control objects. Reaction times, manual dexterity, and arm-hand steadiness are examples of psychomotor abilities. Sensory tests assess candidates' visual, auditory, and speech perception. The ability to speak clearly, discriminate colors, and see in low light conditions are examples of sensory abilities. Physical ability tests assess strength, flexibility, endurance, and coordination. The ability to lift certain amounts of weights, exert yourself physically over extended periods, and keep your balance when in an unstable position are examples of physical abilities. Physical abilities tests can ensure that employees can perform necessary tasks (e.g., firefighters must carry heavy hoses up stairs, delivery people must be able to safely lift and move heavy boxes), and they can help reduce injuries.

Because physical abilities tests can result in adverse impact against women, it is important that all applicants have a fair chance to perform and show that they meet the job's bona fide occupational qualifications or BFOQs. A BFOQ means that the characteristic is essential to the successful performance of a relevant employment function. Only a qualification that affects an employee's ability to perform the job can be considered a BFOQ.[82] BFOQs do not apply to all jobs, and race and color can never be considered BFOQs.

As shown in Table 2 on page 21, when carefully developed to assess relevant job requirements, noncognitive ability tests can be highly valid, well received by applicants, and relatively easy to use.

Values Assessments

There are often key values and core competencies that are tied to business strategy, and it is important to make sure new employees appreciate and share these values. Some companies, including Johnson & Johnson, have improved corporate effectiveness by actively matching individual values to corporate culture.[83] Computerized or paper-and-pencil assessments of candidates' values exist, and some firms try to evaluate them by watching groups of candidates interact on structured tasks and exercises.

One caution about this type of assessment is the fact that applicants' scores on any psychological tests need to be protected.[84] Discuss the use of any psychological test with a qualified lawyer and assess its compliance with the Americans with Disabilities Act (ADA) and other laws.[85] Except in certain situations, if an assessment reveals anything about an employee's mental impairment or a psychological condition, even if it is unintentional, the ADA has been violated.[86]

Personality Assessments

Personality has had a spotty reputation as a predictor of work outcomes. Until the 1990s, personality assessments were a poor predictor of performance.[87] Some of the early tests that were tried were designed for employment screening, but others were originally intended for diagnosing mental illness. The Minnesota Multiphasic Personality Inventory

(MMPI) and California Psychological Inventories presented applicants with true/false questions, including:[88]

- I believe my sins are unpardonable.
- I would like to be a florist.
- Evil spirits possess me sometimes.
- I have no difficulty starting or holding my bowel movement.
- I feel sure there is only one true religion.
- I go to church almost every week.

Given questions like these, it is not surprising that their ability to predict job success was among the lowest of any assessment method. Fortunately, research on the use of personality in predicting job success continued. Because hundreds of different personality traits exist, researchers combined related personality traits and reduced this list into a few broad behavioral (rather than emotional or cognitive) traits that each encompasses many more specific traits. As a group, these five factors of personality capture up to 75 percent of an individual's personality.[89] The five factors are:

1. *Extraversion:* outgoing, assertive, upbeat, and talkative; predicts salesperson performance;[90]
2. *Conscientiousness:* planful, attentive to detail, willing to follow rules and exert effort; predicts performance across all occupations;[91]
3. *Emotional stability:* calm, optimistic, well adjusted, able to allocate resources to accomplish tasks; predicts job performance in most occupations, particularly those involving interpersonal interactions and teamwork such as management, sales,[92] and teaching;[93]
4. *Agreeableness:* sympathetic, friendly, cooperative; predicts performance in jobs involving teamwork and interpersonal interactions;[94] and
5. *Openness to experience:* imaginative, intellectually curious, open to new ideas and change; predicts creativity and expatriate performance.[95]

Conscientiousness and emotional stability seem to predict overall performance for a wide range of jobs.[96] These two "generalizable" traits are measures of trait-oriented work motivation, and seem to affect performance through "will do" motivational components. On the other hand, general mental ability affects performance in all jobs primarily through "can do" capabilities.[97] Extraversion, agreeableness, and openness to experience are valid predictors of performance only in specific occupations or for some criteria.[98] Extraversion predicts performance in occupations where a significant portion of the job involves interacting with others, particularly when influencing others and obtaining status and power is required, such as in managerial and sales jobs.[99] Agreeableness predicts performance in jobs involving significant interpersonal interaction involving helping, cooperating, and nurturing others. Agreeableness may be the single best personality predictor of working well in a team.[100] Employees who are argumentative, inflexible, uncooperative, uncaring, intolerant, and disagreeable (low in agreeableness) are likely to be less effective at teamwork and also engage in more counterproductive behaviors such as theft. Openness to experience predicts creativity and the ability to adapt to change.[101] Employees who are artistically sensitive, intellectual, curious, polished, original, and independent are likely to deal with change and contribute more to innovation at work.[102]

The five factors are very stable over time, and seem to be determined in part by genetics.[103] As with all personality tests, validity of the five is not strong enough to warrant the selection of applicants based solely on their five factor scores. Personality tests, including the five, tend to have low adverse impact and may be able to alleviate the adverse impact caused by other assessment methods, such as cognitive ability tests.

Because job performance reflects many different behaviors, some scholars feel that broad dispositions such as the five factors might best predict it. Some research has supported this proposition,[104] although the validities of the five traits are relatively low compared to other assessment methods. Conscientiousness is the most consistent predictor of performance across all occupations, with an average validity of 0.31,[105] suggesting that conscientiousness may be a useful assessment method for all jobs.

Some prominent scholars argue that the best criterion-related validities will result from matching specific traits (i.e., traits narrower than the five factors) to specific job-relevant performance dimensions.[106] When choosing a personality assessment, it is critical to match the trait to some aspect of job success in terms of both content and specificity. If a firm wants to predict broadly defined job success, such as a global assessment of job performance, broad traits such as the five factors may be better predictors than narrower traits. If the firm wants to predict more specific job success dimensions and work behaviors, such as customer service skills, then narrower traits such as customer service orientation, sales drive, and social interests[107] might have higher validity.

Faking can be an issue with personality assessments, although there is some evidence that applicants who try to enhance their personality test responses also try to manage other's impressions of them on the job, which can actually help them perform the job better.[108] When considering using any personality or values assessment, it is important to assess the test's validity and adverse impact. No personality test will work for all jobs or for every company. How the assessment has held up to any legal challenges is also important, as are applicant reactions to its use. Buros Institute of Mental Measurements publishes a *Mental Measurements Yearbook*[109] that reviews a variety of commercially available cognitive ability (as well as personality and other types of assessment) tests.

Applicant reactions to personality tests tend to be somewhat unfavorable, although drug users have been found to react more negatively than nonusers.[110] The biggest legal problem with personality tests is based on privacy issues, especially if they ask about invasive topics such as religious beliefs and sexual preferences that are not shown to be related to job success or to the job requirement being predicted.[111] Psychological assessments designed for clinical or diagnostic use, such as the MMPI and California Psychological Inventories, should not be used (with the exception of jobs that could endanger public safety, such as police officers, fire fighters, and airline pilots). The courts have consistently ruled against the general use of clinical psychological assessments in the business environment.[112] The use of clinical personality instruments is also inconsistent with the Americans with Disabilities Act (ADA) because they are designed to diagnose abnormal behavioral patterns. The

ADA states that an employer "shall not conduct a medical examination or make inquiries as to whether such applicant is an individual with a disability or as to the nature and severity of such disability." As shown in Table 2 on page 21, personality tests can have low to moderate validity (ranging from -0.13 to 0.33), which improves when the personality assessment is well matched to job criteria. Personality tests are easy to use, but may not be well received by applicants due to a lack of perceived job-relatedness.

Integrity Tests

Why is integrity important? U.S. stores lose billions of dollars each year to shoplifting and employee theft.[113] Hiring employees less likely to steal or engage in other illegal or counterproductive behaviors can be particularly important for jobs requiring money handling such as clerk, teller, or cashier; handling controlled substances; and for security workers and police officers. Integrity tests are typically written tests that use multiple-choice or true/false questions to measure candidates' attitudes and experiences related to their trustworthiness, honesty, moral character, and reliability. Integrity tests can be *clear purpose* and openly assess integrity (sample question: Did you ever write a check knowing you did not have enough money in the bank to cover it?), or *general purpose* and indirectly assess integrity (sample question: Do you like to take chances?).[114]

Integrity tests do not tend to result in adverse impact and appear to be unrelated to cognitive ability. Accordingly, when used with cognitive ability tests, integrity tests can add value in predicting job performance and reduce the adverse impact of the cognitive ability test. Faking also does not appear to be a problem with integrity tests, perhaps because any faking that does occur does not severely impair the validity of the test or because dishonest applicants choose not to fake any more than do honest applicants because they feel that everyone is dishonest and they respond based on what they think everyone does.[115]

As shown in Table 2, the validity of integrity tests averages 0.41 in predicting job performance. For counterproductive work behaviors, the validity of *clear purpose* integrity tests (0.55) is higher than the validity of *general purpose* tests (0.32).[116] Integrity tests predict the broader criterion of counterproductive behaviors, including absenteeism and disciplinary problems, better than they predict employee theft alone.[117] Applicants tend to react somewhat unfavorably to integrity tests,[118] although nondrug users have been found to react more favorably than drug users.[119]

Another issue with integrity tests that applies to all assessment methods is ethical in nature. Some of the people who score poorly on integrity tests are misclassified and wouldn't have stolen from the company. Managers must decide if it is fair or ethical to use a test that incorrectly screens out good applicants.

Integrity tests are relatively inexpensive and can be administered any time during the hiring process. Some companies screen all prospective applicants with integrity tests, and others only screen finalists.[120] As with any assessment method, check the effectiveness of integrity tests in predicting desired work outcomes, including absenteeism, theft, and disciplinary problems, before making them part of the assessment process. Not all commercially available tests have been properly validated following the American Psychological Association's guidelines for using integrity tests.[121] Because theft is not a problem for all companies, sometimes the cost of integrity testing and the small gains in reduced theft are outweighed by the costs of recruiting applicants to replace those screened out by the integrity test.[122] Applicants' privacy rights also need to be protected when administering integrity tests, as with any assessment.

Polygraph Tests

A polygraph test measures and records physiological factors thought to be indicators of anxiety, including blood pressure, respiration, pulse, and skin conductivity while the candidate answers a series of questions. Because anxiety often accompanies the telling of lies, polygraphs are thought to assess lying and honesty. However, if the person is anxious for other reasons, or can voluntarily control his or her anxiety level, conclusions are unreliable. The Polygraph Protection Act prohibits employers from requiring applicants or employees to take a polygraph test, using polygraph results for any employment decision, and discharging or disciplining anyone who refuses to take a polygraph. The only exceptions are for private security firms, controlled substance manufacturers, and during theft, embezzlement, or sabotage investigations that resulted in economic loss or injury to the employer.[123]

Job Knowledge Tests

Job knowledge tests measure the knowledge (often technical) required by a job. These tests are often in multiple-choice, essay, or checklist format and can assess either the candidate's knowledge of job duties or the candidate's knowledge about and level of experience with important job tasks, tools, and processes. An example is a test assessing a HR job applicant's knowledge of human resources. As shown in Table 2 on page 21, job knowledge tests generally result in minimal adverse impact and can be highly valid (average validity of 0.48), particularly for complex jobs.[124] Many firms use job knowledge tests for jobs including correctional officers, maintenance workers, and technical positions.

Interviews

Interviews can assess a variety of skills, abilities, and styles, including communication skills, interpersonal skills, and leadership style. Applicants react very well to interviews, and job seekers often rate interviews as the most job-related selection procedure.[125] In addition to evaluating job applicants, interviews can also serve an important recruiting purpose and communicate information about the job and organization to applicants. Because applicants choose organizations as much as organizations choose applicants, applicants need to receive the information they need to make an informed decision about joining the firm. It is difficult for a single interview to meet both assessment and recruiting goals, perhaps because applicants being assessed are too distracted to focus on the recruiting information being conveyed. Applicants learn more about a job and organization during an interview focused only on recruitment than they do from an interview that tries to accomplish both recruitment and selection goals.[126] Thus, if a company decides to use interviews for recruiting purposes, these interviews should ideally focus exclusively on recruiting.

Doubletree Hotels used the results of interviews with 300 high- and low-performing employees and began screening candidates on the "dimensions of success" it identified. Based on interviews with reservation agents, Doubletree identified seven dimensions for success on the job: practical learning, teamwork, tolerance for stress, sales ability, attention to detail, adaptability/flexibility, and motivation. Doubletree then designed specific interview questions to probe for these and other attributes.[127]

There are several types of interviews used for candidate assessment, and we next discuss some of the most common: unstructured interviews, structured interviews, behavioral interviews, and situational interviews.

Unstructured interviews ask questions that vary from candidate to candidate and that differ across interviewers. There are typically no standards for scoring or evaluating candidates' answers, and they are not always highly job-related. The interview questions are often casual and open-ended (e.g., "tell me about yourself") and can be highly speculative (e.g., "What do you see yourself doing in 5-10 years?"). The interviewer often relies on his or her personal theories about what makes someone a good hire, such as personal appearance and nonverbal cues (e.g., fidgeting and making eye contact), and makes a quick global evaluation of the candidate when the interview has finished. As shown in Table 2, the reliability of unstructured interviews can be low (averaging 0.20 to 0.38) due to their lack of consistency, which reduces their validity. Many managers like using unstructured interviews because they feel that they are good judges of others, or believe that they have devised clever (although unvalidated) ways of verbally evaluating candidates. Given their expense and the legal risks associated with asking nonstandardized questions that have not been validated or shown to be related to job success, it is hard to recommend unstructured interviews.

Interview time can be better spent asking standardized, valid questions shown to predict job success. A structured interview is "a series of job-related questions with predetermined answers that are consistently applied across all interviews for a particular job."[128] Structured interviews use a standardized set of questions and a formal scoring system for candidates' answers to assess a variety of skills and abilities, including communication skills, interpersonal skills, leadership style, etc. The questions are based on a job analysis, making them job-related and well received by applicants. Because the same questions are asked in the same way for all applicants, and because raters are trained to consistently use the same rating scale to evaluate answers, structured interviews tend to have good reliability and validity. Structured interviews have three characteristics:

1. All applicants are asked the same questions;
2. Questions are systematically developed to assess specific job-relevant qualifications; and
3. A formal scoring system is used to evaluate answers.

Structured interviews of all types help to reduce distortions caused by interviewer bias, differences in questions posed to applicants, and unrelated factors such as physical attractiveness, fidgeting, style of dress, etc. As shown in Table 2, structured interviews have an average validity of as high as 0.63, and are liked by applicants. They can be moderately expensive to develop, and interviewers need to be trained in their use. Structured interviews are correlated with cognitive ability, and can generate disparate impact. Table 6 outlines the steps involved in crafting a structured interview.

Table 6. Steps in Crafting a Structured Interview

1. For the job requirements to be measured by a structured interview, identify the actions and behaviors that illustrate each qualification. For example, what does "leadership skills" mean in the context of the job being filled? What do people with good and bad leadership skills do? What is the impact of different leadership strategies? Are different leadership approaches equally effective?
2. Write questions that will generate relevant information about the degree to which candidates' possess each job requirement.
3. Create an answer key with benchmark responses for at least the high, middle, and low scores on the scale.
4. Weight the benchmark responses based on the importance of each question relative to the others. Give more important questions greater weight relative to the other questions.
5. Select and train interviewers to increase standardization, reliability, and validity.
6. Evaluate the effectiveness of the structured interview in terms of validity and stakeholder reactions, including perceived fairness and job-relatedness.

There are two types of structured interviews: behavioral and situational. The choice of behavioral or situational interview questions depends on the person's level of prior work experience. When interviewing people with limited work experience, situational ("what would you do if …") questions are likely to generate more insightful answers than behavioral questions ("what did you do when …"). We discuss behavioral and situational interviews in more detail next.

Behavioral interviews are based on the idea that what an applicant has *done* is a better indicator of future job success than what the applicant believes, feels, thinks, or knows. They assume that past behavior is a good predictor of future behavior.[129]

Interviewers first ask a candidate to describe a problem or situation they have faced at work, during volunteer or public service work, or any other relevant situation that highlights a particular skill, trait or core competency. Then the candidate describes the action he or she took and the results it generated. For example, to assess leadership skills a candidate can be asked to describe an ineffective team she was on, what action she took, and what results she obtained. Table 7 shows an example of a behavioral interview question and scoring key.

Table 7. Behavioral Interview Question Assessing Persistence

Question: Tell me about a time when you were working on a project that you felt was important but that others thought was a waste of time. What did you do and what was the result?

5—Excellent: I pursued the project despite obstacles because I really believed in it. I wanted the project to succeed and I tried to find ways around problems.

4

3—Marginal: I continued working on the project but shifted my focus to other projects that had higher probabilities of success.

2

1—Poor: Once I felt that the project had low support I stopped working on it.

Interviewees rarely give the exact answers suggested in the benchmark responses, but training helps interviewers use the benchmarks to determine how to score an applicant's actual answer. Interviewers should be chosen based on their ability to accurately communicate the questions and evaluate candidates' answers, and they should be trained in using the technique. Interviewers need to present the questions in the same way to everyone and consistently score each answer. If a candidate has a limited work history or is just unable to come up with an appropriate situation or problem, it can take skilled probing to obtain a scorable response. Behavioral interviews are most useful in evaluating job candidates who have employment experience, but can also be effective in assessing candidates with little or no work experience. Factors such as work ethic, temperament, values, and general compatibility with the organization can often be assessed in behavioral interviews.

McDonald's believes that a well-run interview can identify an applicant's potential to be a successful McDonald's employee committed to excel in delivering outstanding service. McDonald's uses an interview guide that helps to predict how an applicant's past behavior is likely to influence his or her future performance. The questions look for actual events or situations the candidate has faced rather than allowing applicants to give a general or theoretical response. The interviewer rates candidates on their responses and offers jobs to those who earn the highest ratings.[130]

Many companies use situational interviews, asking people not about past behaviors but about how they might react to hypothetical situations and how they exemplify core values.[131] Situational interviews have fairly high validities, but are often slightly less valid than behavioral interviews.[132] Southwest Airlines often asks prospective employees how they recently used their sense of humor in a work environment and how they have used humor to defuse a difficult situation. Southwest also looks for humor in the interaction people have with each other during group interviews.[133]

One caution about behavioral and situational interviews is warranted. Web sites, including Vault.com and WetFeet.com, provide extensive information about companies' recruiting and hiring processes, actual interview questions, and summaries of the firms and their cultures. Companies' own web sites often describe the qualities they are looking for in new hires and what it takes to fit into their cultures. These resources make it possible for some job seekers to fabricate answers to anticipated interview questions.

How can an employer spot false stories and improve the validity of its behavioral interviews? Asking follow-up questions, curiously requesting more specific information about the story, asking the candidate what he or she was thinking or feeling at the time, and asking what the candidate learned from the experience can make it more difficult for the candidate to maintain a consistent story.[134]

Structured, behavioral, and situational interviewing applies a planned and validated scoring system to each interview question. When interview questions are developed, job experts also create a rating scale for a continuum of possible answers, ranging from excellent to poor, that link directly to behavioral objectives determined in the job analysis. Excellent answers indicate probable success, marginal answers reflect probable difficulty, and poor answers indicate probable failure in performing the related job task. Although the exact expert-generated answers are rarely given, interviewers are trained to score their responses meaningfully at some point on the continuum marked by these anchors. Table 8 illustrates a behavioral interview rating scale that can be adapted for any type of structured interview.

Table 8. Situational Interview Scoring Key—Assessing Communication Skills

Question: Imagine that you are currently very busy working on several important projects with firm deadlines, but your supervisor brings you a stack of paperwork to complete that you feel is unrelated to any of your projects. In addition, you are certain that attending to this new paperwork will cause you to miss several project deadlines. What would you do?

5—*Excellent:* Explain the conflict to my supervisor and try to identify and discuss alternatives. It would be important to me to ensure that any changes were acceptable to both my manager and me.

4

3—*Marginal:* Tell my supervisor about the conflict.

2

1—*Poor:* Accept the conflict as part of the job and do the best I can.

Situational Judgment Tests

Situational judgment tests measure job candidates' noncognitive skills. Short scenarios are presented verbally, in writing, or in videos, and candidates are asked what they believe is the most effective response, or choose the best response from a list of alternatives. The FBI uses situational judgment tests to measure candidates' ability to organize, plan, and prioritize, relate effectively with others, maintain a positive image, evaluate information and make judgment decisions, adapt to changing situations, and integrity.[135] Situational judgment tests are similar to situational interviews but may also be paper-and-pencil based. They tend to have moderate validity of about 0.34.

Graphology

Some employers use handwriting analysis in staffing decisions. Graphology includes any practice which involves determining personality traits or abilities from a person's handwriting. In 1996, about 6,000 American companies reported using graphology. The real number may be higher because many companies use, but do not admit to using, the technique.[136] We do not recommend graphology as an assessment method as it has been found to have little or no validity[137] and applicants tend to find it invasive.[138]

Other strong arguments against using graphology in employment decisions at all include concerns about ethics, privacy, and courts' traditional hostility to graphology.[139] Because graphology may discriminate against job applicants and employees with physical and emotional handicaps, it may also violate the Americans with Disabilities Act (ADA).[140] A good rule of thumb is that if an individual who has an ADA-defined disability cannot take a test, then it should not be used unless it can be adapted for use by those individuals. Handwriting analysis clearly falls into the group of tests that cannot be adapted to be administered to individuals who fall within one or more ADA-defined disabilities.

Job Simulations

Many job candidates look good on paper or during interviews, but can they really perform the job successfully? Past job performance would be great to know, but can be difficult to learn. Job simulations measure job skills (e.g., programming or engine repair skills) using candidate performance on tasks similar to those performed on the job. Simulations can be *verbal*, requiring interpersonal interaction and language skills such as a role-playing test for a call center worker. *Motor* simulations involve the physical manipulation of things, such as an assembly task or a test to see if a candidate can properly operate a machine. Multiple, trained raters and detailed rating systems are typically used to evaluate and score behaviors and performance.

Simulations also differ in their degree of *fidelity*, or the similarity between the scenario and the actual job tasks. The highest fidelity tests (like flight simulators) use very realistic and often expensive equipment and scenarios to simulate actual job tasks and situations. In high-fidelity tests, candidates actually do the work. Low-fidelity tests simulate the task in a written or verbal statement, and candidates respond verbally or in writing. Behavioral interviews can be a type of verbal, low-fidelity simulation. Simulations can be highly valid (averaging 0.54) and generally result in minimal adverse impact. Job candidates also tend to like them because they are highly job-related. Because of their expense, particularly for high-fidelity simulations, some firms choose to use simulations later in the assessment process after the pool of applicants has been reduced. If a company plans to train new employees, then simulations may be less appropriate. The use of simulations is rising, particularly in manufacturing, sales, health care, and call centers.[141]

L'Oréal uses an online assessment that simulates real-world market conditions. Student teams log on to the Internet and "become" general managers of a cosmetics company. They decide how much to invest in research and development, how much to spend on marketing, and find ways to cut production costs without compromising quality. The game responds to every move by showing players their decisions' impact on their virtual company's share price. In the first four years it used the simulation, L'Oréal hired 186 top players from 28 countries.[142]

Prudential Realty uses a simulation that shows videos of actors posing as homebuyers. The actors "talk" to the aspiring realtors, who then choose from a list what they consider the best response to the situation. Prudential feels that it can teach new real estate agents sales skills, but they still need certain personality traits to succeed in the business. The simulation reveals whether job applicants have those traits or not. In their first year, high scoring agents earned over 300 percent more than those who scored low.[143] Simulations can also serve as a recruiting tool—one real estate firm places a monthly newspaper ad that states, "Test Drive a Career in Real Estate Today" and directs readers to the company's web site to do a simulation.[144]

Because they seem so job relevant, it can be tempting to overweigh simulations in making screening decisions and ignore other components of the recruitment process. Experts recommend balancing simulation results with interviews, written assessment tests, and reference and background checks. No matter how well Prudential job applicants perform on the realtor simulation, they must still do well at an interview. At

L'Oréal, the top performing teams make a presentation to a panel of judges during which they explain their business strategy and try to convince L'Oréal to invest in their fictitious company. The presentation helps L'Oréal assess candidates' personalities and communication skills.[145] Depending on their cost, simulations may be used earlier in the assessment process. More expensive simulations may be reserved for use later in the assessment process on a smaller group of candidates.

Work Samples

Work samples require a candidate to perform observable work tasks or job-related behaviors to predict future job success. Work samples can include simulations, giving candidates an actual job task to perform, or even probationary hiring. Work samples can also simulate critical events that might occur on the job to assess how well a candidate handles them. A candidate for a 9-1-1 dispatch center might be asked to handle calls from distraught people and handle a high volume of calls to assess how they respond. These work samples can also take the form of a picture or description of an incident. A candidate then responds to a series of questions and indicates the decisions he or she would make and actions he or she would take. Job experts then score the test. Although they can be expensive to develop and administer, particularly in the case of probationary hiring, work samples tend to be highly reliable and can have high validity and low adverse impact, if done well.

Work samples do not measure applicants' aptitudes, only what they are able to do at the current time. Work sample trainability tests provide a candidate with a period of training on the work sample tasks. Training performance is then evaluated by having the candidate perform the work sample. Work sample trainability tests are useful when the company intends to extensively train new hires.

As shown in Table 2 on page 21, work samples have an average validity of 0.33, low adverse impact, and are generally received well by applicants. Work samples are most useful for jobs and work tasks that can be completed in a short period, and are less able to predict performance on jobs where tasks may take days or weeks to complete. The difficulty of faking job proficiency helps to increase the validity of work samples. Work samples can often be content validated for some jobs when the person can demonstrate or provide a portfolio of related achievements he or she would be expected to produce in the target job.

Assessment centers that put candidates through a variety of simulations and assessments to evaluate their potential fit with and ability to do the job are one type of work sample. As shown in Table 2, assessment centers have an average validity of 0.37 and low adverse impact, although they tend to be expensive and one of the more difficult assessment methods to use.

To assess leadership, Southwest Airlines has used a group assessment exercise called Fallout Shelter, in which flight attendant candidates imagine they are a committee charged with rebuilding civilization after a just-declared nuclear war. Groups are given a list of 15 people from different occupations, including nurse, teacher, all-sport athlete, biochemist, and pop singer and have 10 minutes to make a unanimous decision about which seven people can remain in the only available fallout shelter. As the candidates propose, discuss, and debate, each is graded on a scale ranging from "passive" to "active" to "leader."[146]

Reference Checks

Reference checks can reveal information about a candidate's past performance or measure the accuracy of the statements a candidate makes in an interview or on his or her resume. Individuals with previous experience with the job candidate, usually people referred by the job candidate, are asked to provide confirmation of a candidate's statements or an evaluation of the job candidate. Although many previous employers are unwilling to provide extensive information about a candidate due to risks of a defamation lawsuit, references should still be contacted as not checking references increases the risk of negligent hiring. Current employees may even be located who have worked with the candidate in the past and can provide useful information. Rather than asking general questions about the candidate, asking references for relevant information about the indicators of success that you have established for the job can generate useful information, as can asking questions about the types of situations and work environments in which the candidate would excel.

The laws and protections for employers doing reference checks differ by state. Some states, including Wisconsin, have very broad protection for employers to give factual information in reference checks. Because other states are less employer-friendly, it is wise to become familiar with local laws and protections. Reference checks have low adverse impact but have a relatively low average validity of 0.26, which could likely be greater if references were willing to share more candid information without fear of being sued. Applicants generally expect reference checks as a part of the hiring process.

Sometimes more detailed questions can get a better response from reluctant references. One expert suggests setting up scenarios so the supervisor can better understand the context of your question, such as:[147]

- I'm wondering what kind of environment would be the best fit for Kim. Do you recommend a more structured environment, with clear guidelines and close supervision, or would she excel in a more self-directed culture?
- Some people constantly reinvent their jobs and willingly assume responsibilities beyond their job description. Other people are only interested in performing their job duties and little else. Can you tell me where Manuel fits on that continuum?
- We often struggle to find the ideal balance between quality and production. If John leaned in one direction more than the other, would you say it was toward quality or quantity?

Although many companies use reference checks as a contingent assessment method, it can be helpful to contact a person's references earlier in the assessment process to acquire valuable information about a candidate's previous work responsibilities and performance, help rank candidates, and assist in making your final decision. It is a good idea to check at least three references for each candidate, with one of those three being a direct supervisor.

Contingent Assessment Methods

Contingent assessments are performed after a job offer has been extended to the candidate. The offer is made contingent on the person passing the contingent assessment.

Medical and Drug Tests

Because of the potential to violate applicants' privacy and the importance of legal compliance, use medical tests, including drug tests, with great care. Medical exams are usually used to identify a job candidate's potential health risks, and must assess only job-related factors consistent with business necessity.[148] Medical information should be consistently assessed for all entering employees in the same job category, regardless of disability.[149] The ADA regulates the use of medical exams to prevent employers from screening out individuals with disabilities for reasons unrelated to job performance. A survey investigating new-hire medical testing found that 60 percent of the U.S. firms surveyed required medical exams for at least some jobs.[150] The most common medical test used is drug testing, and the most frequently given reason for drug testing is to establish an applicant's ability to perform assigned job tasks.[151]

Genetic testing is a type of testing that can identify people genetically susceptible to certain diseases that could result from exposure to toxic substances in the workplace such as chemicals or radiation. Although some companies have experimented with genetic screening, with the passage of the Genetic Information Nondiscrimination Act of 2008 (GINA), it is now illegal to deny U.S. citizens jobs simply because they have an inherited illness, or a genetic predisposition to a particular disease.[152]

Any medical information obtained should be kept confidential and stored separately from other applicant and employee files.[153] Medical tests can be administered only after all other application components have been cleared and a job offer has been extended. Only by making the job offer contingent on passing the drug or other medical test is it possible for an applicant to tell whether he or she was rejected on the basis of a disability and not because of insufficient skills or experience.

The timing of a medical test is critical. Some companies find themselves in legal trouble just for failing to follow the required legal sequence. One company had not completed the background checks on some of its applicants before asking them to take medical and blood tests. When some of these individuals were found to be HIV-positive but had not revealed it prior to the medical exam, the company rescinded the offers that had been made, citing that the applicants had not been forthright about their condition. Three candidates sued the company and the court determined that it did not matter whether the candidates had been forthright about their health condition. The court concluded that administering the medical tests before the background check was complete made it difficult for the applicants to determine whether they had been denied employment because of issues with their background checks or with their physical exam.[154] The court made it clear that an applicant's medical information should be the last information collected after making a contingent job offer.

Drug tests are an assessment method that has generated great debate. Opponents of drug testing often cite privacy concerns, issues related to drug tests wrongly identifying someone as having drugs in his or her system ("false positives"), and numerous studies questioning the cost-effectiveness of drug tests. On the other hand, the cost of drug and alcohol abuse costs employers billions of dollars every year. Some of the costs of employee drug and alcohol abuse are obvious (e.g., increased absences, accidents, and errors), but less obvious costs—including low employee morale, increased health care costs, increased workers' compensation claims, and higher turnover—can be equally harmful.[155]

Drug testing is not required under the Drug-Free Workplace Act of 1988. Although many state and local governments have statutes that limit or prohibit workplace testing unless required by state or federal regulations for certain jobs, most private employers have the right to test for a wide variety of illegal substances. Familiarizing yourself with all relevant state and federal regulations that apply to your organization is essential before designing a drug-testing program,[156] and some collective bargaining agreements also impact drug testing policies.

A clear drug testing policy should be in place before conducting the tests, and applicants should be informed of the policy. Policy issues include who will be tested, the consequences of a positive test, what substances will be tested for, when testing will be conducted, cutoff levels, safeguards, and confirmation procedures. The Department of Labor has online tools and information to help employers develop sound drug testing policies and effective, balanced drug-free workplace programs that go beyond drug testing.[157]

Background Checks

Background checks assess factors including a person's personal and credit characteristics, character, lifestyle, criminal history, and general reputation. Pre-employment background checks for misdemeanor and felony convictions or other offenses are routine in many industries, including financial services, health care, child care, and elder care. In the United States, criminal records are archived at the county level, requiring a search of criminal records in each county where the job candidate has lived. Because this is burdensome, and because of the legal importance of conducting a thorough background check as a negligent hiring defense, many companies prefer to outsource background checks to qualified firms. Because crimes committed post-hire could contribute to a negligent retention charge, at least one security firm, Verified Person, sends automated biweekly updates that alert a company to any new misdemeanor or felony convictions of any of a company's employees.[158]

Organizations are also using online searches to learn about job candidates. Using a search engine like Google.com to find information about a candidate can uncover additional information about them. Job candidates have even been denied job offers due to unprofessional content placed on social networking sites such as Facebook and MySpace.[159] Because much Internet content is archived, employers can access information about a candidate that goes back many years.

Unless a business is involved in national defense or security, background checks must be relevant to the nature of the job and job requirements. Employers must communicate that background checks will be conducted when people apply for a job, and applicants must first give their written consent.[160] Fully document all background check efforts and any contact with former employers, supervisors, and references.

The Fair and Accurate Credit Transactions Act of 2003[161] (FACTA) establishes important reporting and disclosure requirements and covers a wide array of background reports. A job applicant must give written consent before a background check can begin. Employers cannot use negative information that is more than seven years old unless it applies to the hiring of high-profile job candidates who earn $75,000 or more.[162] Any credit data from consumer credit reports must be destroyed after it has fulfilled its "business purpose." [163] The Federal Trade Commission

(FTC) web site (www.ftc.gov) provides more information on the requirements of the FACTA. State requirements generally overrule federal requirements and can be even stricter.

A consumer report contains information about an individual's personal and credit characteristics, character, lifestyle, and general reputation.[164] If they comply with the Fair Credit Reporting Act (FCRA), employers can use consumer reports when hiring new employees and when evaluating employees for promotion, reassignment, and retention. The FCRA protects the privacy of consumer report information and guarantees that the information supplied by consumer reporting agencies is as accurate as possible. Amendments to the FCRA that went into effect September 30, 1997, significantly increase the legal obligations of employers who use consumer reports. Congress expanded employer responsibilities because of concern that inaccurate or incomplete consumer reports could cause applicants to be denied jobs or cause employees to be denied promotions unjustly. The amendments ensure (1) that individuals are aware that consumer reports may be used for employment purposes and agree to such use, and (2) that individuals are notified promptly if information in a consumer report may result in a negative employment decision.[165] To be covered by the FCRA, a report must be prepared by a consumer reporting agency (CRA) that assembles such reports for other businesses. For sensitive positions, employers often order investigative consumer reports that include interviews with an applicant's or employee's friends, neighbors, and associates. All of these types of reports are consumer reports if they are obtained from a CRA.

If negative information is found, the employer must give the job applicant an "adverse action notice" that includes the screening company's name and contact information and explains that the applicant can dispute the information for either accuracy or completeness. Applicants must also be given a fair amount of time to contest the findings.[166] Job seekers can check the accuracy of and correct errors in their background reports and credit histories by researching themselves. MyBackgroundCheck.com and MyJobHistory.com both allow individuals to perform background checks on themselves, and even provide a certificate that verifies their degrees, credit, employment, and criminal history to potential employers.

Improper documentation during background checks exposes an employer to allegations of neglect. When Interim Healthcare of Fort Wayne Inc. was accused of negligent hiring and retention of a home nursing aid, it could not show evidence of having conducted a proper background check on its employee.[167] Fully documenting its background checking efforts may have absolved Interim Healthcare of the accusations.[168]

Importantly, an employer does not have to prove allegations of misconduct leading to an adverse employment decision are true as long as it conducts a proper investigation and acts in good faith on the information that it obtains. Thus, an employer can greatly reduce its potential liability for negligent hiring just by conducting a reasonable background check. Even if an employer is not able to actually obtain any information about a candidate from a previous place of work, going through the investigative process and documenting it well goes a long way in reducing liability.[169] Background checks at the time of hiring should include the accuracy of all stated academic credentials and other information submitted by the applicant and used in making a hiring decision.

Multiple Methods

Most organizations use multiple tools to assess candidates—perhaps a resume screen, an interview, personality or skills assessments, reference and background checks, and some form of simulation. Renda Broadcasting in Pittsburgh, Pennsylvania, regularly hires advertising sales representatives to work in the firm's 25 radio stations. In addition to a three- or four-stage structured interviewing process, candidates make a final presentation to the sales manager and general manager of the station to assess their communication skills before a job offer contingent on background checks and drug screens is made.[170]

Obviously, few assessment methods are appropriate for assessing all important applicant characteristics. For example, low-level jobs, or jobs for which extensive training will be provided after hire, are not good matches for job knowledge tests, and assessment centers may not be appropriate for simple jobs and abilities. Some assessment methods, such as personality tests, may differ in their usefulness for different jobs. Don't neglect applicant reactions to the assessment methods used—applicants who hold positive perceptions about a company's selection processes and view them as fair are more likely to view the company favorably and report stronger intentions to recommend the employer to others and to accept job offers.[171]

Like Southwest Airlines, Nucor Steel uses written tests and in-depth interviews to evaluate job candidates. It also relies on the expertise of industrial psychologists, who frequently visit the company's plants to screen prospects and evaluate employees. Nucor's highly entrepreneurial, extremely performance-oriented, tough culture means that smart minds are more important than big muscles. Because this environment is not for everybody, Nucor works extra hard to find the right people.[172]

Can you imagine receiving a job offer after only a 15-minute interview? What message would that send? A more extensive assessment procedure reflects a concerted effort on the part of the company to match the candidate with a job at which he or she is likely to succeed. A more rigorous assessment procedure tends to impress quality candidates, rather than turning them off to the job and organization.

Reducing Adverse Impact

Some of the most useful assessment methods for predicting job performance, such as cognitive ability tests, often result in adverse impact. Although the courts have ruled that it is not permissible to adjust members of a protected group's scores to reduce the assessment method's adverse impact, there are some strategies to reduce adverse impact.

Although they don't always work, some strategies to reduce adverse impact include:

- Using targeted recruitment to increase the numbers of qualified minority applicants
- Expanding the definition of job performance to include areas of contextual performance such as commitment and reliability in addition to task performance
- Combining predictors can reduce adverse impact, although this does not always work. If a cognitive ability test predicts job performance but discriminates against women, using it in conjunction with another valid assessment method that either does not have any adverse impact based on sex or that discriminates against men can reduce or eliminate the adverse impact of the cognitive ability test.[173]
- Using well-developed simulations rather than cognitive ability tests
- If only a few applicants are ultimately hired (low selection ratio), using assessment methods with less adverse impact early in the selection process and those with greater adverse impact later in the process
- Using banding and assigning the same score to applicants who score in a range on the assessment (think of grades—students scoring from 93 to 100 percent are placed in the A band, those

scoring from 85 to 93 percent are placed into the B band, etc.) and using only the banded score to compare applicants. This technique can reduce an assessment's adverse impact but will also reduce the validity of the test.

Race norming, or adjusting scores on a standardized test by using separate curves for different racial groups, is illegal. Race norming could award a job applicant with a test percentile score of 48 the same test score as an applicant of a different race scoring in the 75th percentile. The Civil Rights Act of 1991 prohibits score adjustments, the use of different score requirements for different groups of test takers, or alteration of employment-related test results based on the demographics of the test takers.

Assessment Plans

Companies use many different methods to assess job candidates. How should a firm choose which to use? The best methods are those that best assess the targeted applicant characteristics or competencies (are valid), that meet the goals of the external assessment process, and that meet the needs of the assessment method's stakeholders. Because different methods are good at assessing different things, usually more than one assessment method is necessary to evaluate all of the important criteria used in making hiring decisions. In fact, because no predictor is perfect and because multiple assessment increases the accuracy of a candidate's evaluation, more than one assessment method should be used in practically every selection situation.

An assessment plan describes which assessment method(s) will be used to assess each of the important characteristics on which applicants will be evaluated, in what sequence the assessments will take place, and what weight each assessment will receive in determining an overall score for that characteristic based on the importance of each characteristic to job performance. Characteristics that will be trained after hire are not assigned to any assessment method, but any existing qualifications required to qualify for the training program should be listed. Table 9 illustrates a possible format of an assessment plan for an accountant. The weights for each assessment method are based on the job-analysis ratings of the relative importance and relative time spent on each dimension.

Which assessment methods are used and when is up to the company and its goals. Sometimes firms use cheaper assessment methods first and more expensive methods later when fewer candidates remain under consideration. To quickly reduce very large candidate pools to a more manageable size, it can make sense to use the lowest cost assessment methods first, or those assessing candidates' abilities to perform

Table 9. Assessment Plan for an Accountant

Characteristic	Importance of Characteristic to Job Performance (1 = most important)	Select (S) Train (T)	Resume
Customer focus	1	S	1 (0.15)
Accounting skills	1	S	1 (0.15)
Budgeting skills	1	S	1 (0.2)
Time management	2	S	
Delegation	2	S	
Ability to use company's accounting software	3	T	
Attention to detail	3	S	

The weights to be given each assessment score are in parentheses next to each number and total 100 percent across each row.

essential job functions. It can also be a good idea to use the most valid assessment methods first, or methods that promote candidate self-selection, prompting people who would likely drop out of the hiring process later to opt out earlier to save the firm time and resources. Some companies require candidates to visit the careers section of their web site before applying to encourage self-screening and reduce the number of poor-quality applicants.

Southwest Airlines is a good example of thoughtful external assessment. Because fun and friendly customer service is essential to the success of Southwest Airlines' business strategy, it takes great care in selecting its flight attendants.[174] Southwest feels that fun counterbalances the stress of hard work. Because it believes that fun is about attitude, Southwest hires for attitude and trains for skills. Southwest believes that it can train new hires on whatever they need to do, but it cannot change people's inherent attitudes.[175] Accordingly, Southwest Airlines looks for the energy, humor, team spirit, and self-confidence that matches its offbeat, creative, customer-focused culture.[176] Job candidates don't just interview for a job, they audition—and the audition starts the moment they call for an application. When a recruit calls, managers jot down anything memorable about the conversation, good or bad. Recruits flown out for interviews receive special tickets that alert gate agents, flight attendants,

Assessment Method and its Sequence in the Assessment Process				
hone Screen	Accounting and Budgeting Test	Recruiter Interview	Simulation	Hiring Manager Interview
2 (0.15)		3 (0.2)	4 (0.25)	5 (0.25)
2 (0.15)	3 (0.4)		4 (0.3)	
2 (0.2)	3 (0.25)		4 (0.35)	
		1 (0.3)	2 (0.4)	3 (0.3)
1 (0.2)		2 (0.4)	3 (0.4)	
1 (0.25)		2 (0.25)	3 (0.50)	

and others to pay special attention. Employees observe whether recruits are consistently friendly to others or complaining and drinking cocktails at 9 a.m., and pass their observations on to the People Department.[177]

Flight attendant recruits are evaluated even when they think that they're not being assessed. When flight attendant applicants give five-minute speeches about themselves in front of as many as 50 other recruits, managers watch the audience as closely as the speaker to see who is enthusiastically supporting their potential co-workers. Unselfish people who will support their teammates are the ones who catch Southwest's eye, not the applicants who seem bored or distracted or use the time to polish their own presentations.[178] Southwest's flight attendant assessment methods not only keep turnover low but also help it execute its customer service strategy. Southwest also consistently receives the lowest number of passenger complaints in the industry.[179]

Referring to Table 9, the numbers under each assessment method indicate the order in which the various assessment methods will be used to assess each characteristic. Reading across the first row, consumer focus is one of the top three characteristics relevant to internal accountants' job performance, and it will be assessed rather than trained post-hire. Consumer focus is first assessed via a resume scan, then through a phone screen. A recruiter interview, simulation performance, and hiring manager interview then further assess each candidate's customer focus. In combining each of the assessment scores into one rating for each characteristic, weights are given to each assessment score (shown in parentheses next to each number) that total 100 percent for each characteristic being assessed. In this case, customer focus assessed via the resume and phone screen will each be weighted 0.15, assessed via the recruiter interview will be weighted 0.2, via the simulation 0.25, and via the manager interview 0.25. In determining an overall candidate score that can be used to compare candidates, each characteristic is weighted based on its importance to job performance (based on the relative importance and relative time spent information about each job duty collected during the job analysis). In this case, the characteristics rated 1 in importance might each be weighted 0.20, those rated 2 might each be weighted 0.15, and the one rated 3 might be weighted 0.1.

Summary

The primary goal of external candidate assessment is typically identifying the job candidates who fit the person specification for the job being filled, and to identify people who would likely be poor performers and screen them out. The assessment system should also evaluate candidates' fit with the organization, group, and supervisor, and their ability to contribute to business strategy execution. This allows a firm to identify the job candidates best able to perform the open job and best able to help the company execute its business strategy and enhance its competitive advantage.

There are a variety of important goals organizations have when assessing external job candidates, including return on investment, shareholder reactions, establishing and reinforcing the firm's employer image, and complying with legal requirements by using valid assessment methods in a fair, consistent, and objective manner.

Companies can choose from many different assessment methods to assess job candidates. The choice should be based on which methods best assess the applicant characteristics or competencies identified as important during the job analysis as well as the ability of the assessment method to meet other important goals of the external assessment process. Because different methods are good at assessing different things, and differ in their cost, validity, applicant reactions, and adverse impact, it is often necessary to use more than one assessment method. Just because an assessment method results in adverse impact, if it does a good job predicting job performance, it may be worthwhile to investigate the usefulness of various strategies to reduce its adverse impact so that it can continue to be used.

Endnotes

[1] See Phillips, J.M. & Gully, S.M. *Strategic Staffing*, 2009. Upper Saddle River, NJ: Prentice Hall.

[2] Kelley, R. & Caplan, J., "How Bell Labs Create Star Performers," *Harvard Business Review*, July-August 1993, pp. 128-139; DeMarco, T. & Lister, T., *Peopleware: Productive Projects and Teams*, 1987, New York: Dorset House Publishing Company, p. 44.

[3] Donnelly, G. (2000). Recruiting, retention, and returns. *CFO Magazine*, March.

[4] Palmeri, C., "The Fastest Drill in the West," *BusinessWeek*, October 24, 2005, 86-88.

[5] Poe, A.C., "Graduate Work: Behavioral Interviewing Can Tell You if an Applicant Just Out of College Has Traits Needed for the Job," October 2003, 48(10), available online at: http://www.shrm.org/hrmagazine/articles/1003/1003poe. asp. Accessed January 4, 2009.

[6] Rosensweig, D., "What I Know Now," *Fast Company*, February 2005, p. 96.

[7] Overman, S., "With Economic Recovery Predicted, Companies Should Sharpen Recruiting Skills Now," Society for Human Resource Management Online, November 24, 2003, available online at: http://www.shrm.org/hrnews_ published/archives/CMS_006419.asp. August 8, 2008.

[8] Carbonara, P., "Hire for Attitude, Train for Skill," *Fast Company*, August 1996, 4, p. 73.

[9] For a more extensive discussion, see Kristof-Brown, A.L., Zimmerman, R.D., and Johnson, E.C., "Consequences of Individuals' Fit at Work: A Meta-analysis of Person-job, Person-organization, Person-group, and Person-supervisor Fit," *Personnel Psychology*, 2005, 58, 281-342.

[10] Adapted from Edwards, J.R., "Person-job Fit: A Conceptual Integration, Literature Review, and Methodological Critique," In C.L. Cooper and I.T. Robertson (eds.), *International Review of Industrial and Organizational Psychology*, (Vol. 6), 1991, 283-357. New York: Wiley.

[11] Caldwell, D.F. & O'Reilly, C.A., "Measuring Person-job Fit Within a Profile Comparison Process," *Journal of Applied Psychology*, 1990, 75, 648-657; Edwards, J.R., "Person-job Fit: A Conceptual Integration, Literature Review, and Methodological Critique," In C.L. Cooper and I.T. Robertson (eds.), *International Review of Industrial and Organizational Psychology*, (Vol. 6), 1991, 283-357. New York: Wiley.

[12] Delaney, K.J., "Google Adjusts Hiring Process as Needs Grow," *The Wall Street Journal*, October 23, 2006, p. B1.

[13] Kristof-Brown, A.L., Zimmerman, R.D., and Johnson, E.C., "Consequences of Individuals' Fit at Work: A Meta-analysis of Person-job, Person-organization, Person-group, and Person-supervisor fit," *Personnel Psychology*, 2005, 58, 281-342.

[14] Ibid.

[15] Werbel, J.D. & Gilliland, S.W., "Person-environment Fit in the Selection Process," In G.R. Ferris (ed.), *Research in Personnel and Human Resource Management*, Vol. 17, 1999, 209-243. Stamford, CT: JAI Press.

[16] Peter Sinton, "Teamwork the Name of the Game for Ideo," *San Francisco Chronicle*, February 23, 2000, available online at: http://www.sfgate.com/cgi-bin/article.cgi?file=/chronicle/archive/2000/02/23/BU39355.DTL.

[17] Kristof, A.L., "Person-organization Fit: An Integrative Review of its Conceptualizations, Measurement, and Implications," *Personnel Psychology*, 1996, 49, 1-50.; Kristof, A.L., "Perceived Applicant Fit: Distinguishing Between Recruiters' Perceptions of Person-job and Person-organization Fit," *Personnel Psychology*, 2000, 53, 643-671.

[18] E.g., Chatman, J., "Improving Interactional Organizational Research: A Model of Person-organization Fit," *Academy of Management Review*, 1989, 14, 333-349; Chatman, J., "Matching People and Organizations: Selection and Socialization in Public Accounting Firms," *Administrative Science Quarterly*, 1991, 36, 459-484; Vancouver, J.B. & Schmitt. N.W., "An Exploratory Examination of Person-organization Fit: Organizational Goal Congruence," *Personnel Psychology*, 1991, 44, 333-352.

[19] Kristof-Brown, A.L., Zimmerman, R.D., and Johnson, E.C., "Consequences of Individuals' Fit at Work: A Meta-analysis of Person-job, Person-organization, Person-group, and Person-supervisor fit," *Personnel Psychology*, 2005, 58, 281-342.

[20] Ibid.

[21] O'Reilly, C.A. III, Chatman, J., & Caldwell, D.V., "People and Organizational Culture: A Profile Comparison Approach to Assessing Person-organization Fit," *Academy of Management Journal*, 1991, 34, 487-516.

[22] Ashford, S.J. & Taylor, M.S., "Adaptations to Work Transitions: An Integrative Approach," In G. Ferris & K. Rowland (eds.) *Research in Personnel and Human Resources Management*, 1990, vol. 8, pp. 1-39.

[23] Available online at: www.jnj.com.

[24] Michaels, L., "The HR Side of Competitive Advantage," *Thunderbird Magazine*, 2002, 55 (1).

[25] Weber, G., "The Recruiting Payoff of Social Responsibility," *Workforce Management* Online, January 2005, available online at: http://www.workforce.com/section/06/article/23/93/45.html. Accessed February 16, 2009.

[26] Holland, J.L., *Making Vocational Choices: A Theory of Vocation Personalities and Work Environments*, 1985, Englewood Cliffs, NJ: Prentice-Hall.

[27] Muchinsky, P.M. & Monahan, C.J., "What is person-environment congruence? Supplementary versus complementary models of fit," *Journal of Vocational Behavior*, 1987, 31, 268-77.

[28] Ibid, 269.

[29] Anders, G., "Talent Bank," *Fast Company*, June 2000, 94.

[30] Muchinsky, P.M. & Monahan, C.J., "What is person-environment congruence? Supplementary versus complementary models of fit," *Journal of Vocational Behavior*, 1987, 31, 269.

[31] T.A. Judge & S. Watanabe, "Is the Past Prologue? A Test of Ghiselli's Hobo Syndrome," 1995, *Journal of Management*, 21, 211-29.

[32] Minton-Eversole, T., "Number of Employers Doesn't Always Equate to Hiring Advantage," Society for Human Resource Management Online, December 2006, available online at: http://www.shrm.org/ema/news_published/CMS_019470. asp. Accessed January 22, 2008.

[33] "McDonald's Makes Promise to Value People," IRMA.org, September 16, 2002, available online at: http://www.irma.org/retailersoftheyear/contentview. asp?c=5601. Accessed February 16, 2009.

[34] "Recruiting, Selecting and Training for Success," tt100.biz, available online at: http://www.thetimes100.co.uk/case_study.php?cID=28&csID=194&pID=1. Accessed July 10, 2008.

[35] Tyler, K., "Put Applicants' Skills to the Test," *HR Magazine*, January 2000, pp. 75-7.

[36] *Griggs v. Duke Power Co.*, 401 U.S. 424 (1971).

[37] See http://www.dol.gov/dol/allcfr/Title_41/Part_60-3/toc.htm. Accessed January 29, 2009.

[38] Equal Employment Opportunity Commission, "Uniform Employee Selection Guidelines Interpretation and Clarification (Questions and Answers)," available online at: http://www.uniformguidelines.com/questionandanswers.html. Accessed January 29, 2009.

[39] Uniform Guideline 14C(4), 43 Fed. Reg. 38, 302 (1978).

[40] Available online at: http://www.dol.gov/dol/allcfr/Title_41/Part_60-3/toc. htm.

[41] Available online at: http://siop.org/_Principles/principlesdefault.aspx.

[42] Available online at: http://www.apa.org/science/standards.html.

[43] Hansen, F., "Recruiting on the Right Side of the Law," *Workforce Management* Online, May 2006. Available online at: http://www.workforce.com/section/06/ feature/24/38/12/. Accessed June 30, 2006.

[44] Ibid.

[45] Sahadi, J., "Top 5 Resume Lies," CNN/Money, December 9, 2004, available online at: http://money.cnn.com/2004/11/22/pf/resume_lies/index.htm. Accessed February 2, 2009.

[46] See e.g., Marquez, J., "Radioshack Gaffe Show [sic] Need to Screen Current Employees," *Workforce Management Online*, March 14, 2006. Available online at: http://www.workforce.com/section/00/article/24/29/52.html. Accessed February 4, 2009.

[47] Martinez, M., "Screening for Quality on the Web," *Employment Management Today*, Winter 2004, 9 (1), available online at: http://www.shrm.org/ema/emt/articles/2004/winter04cover.asp. Accessed February 8, 2009.

[48] Marquez, J., "When Brand Alone Isn't Enough," *Workforce Management*, March 13, 2006, p. 1, 39-41. Available online at: http://www.workforce.com/archive/feature/24/29/58/index.php?ht=mcdonald%20s%20mcdonald%20s. Accessed February 8, 2009.

[49] Martinez, M., "Screening for Quality on the Web," *Employment Management Today*, Winter 2004, 9 (1), available online at: http://www.shrm.org/ema/emt/articles/2004/winter04cover.asp. Accessed February 8, 2009.

[50] Ibid.

[51] England, G.W., *Development and Use of Weighted Application Blanks*, 1961, Dubuque, Iowa: W.M.C. Brown.

[52] Kaak, S.R., "The Weighted Application Blank," *Cornell Hotel and Restaurant Administration Quarterly*, 1998, 39 (2), 18-24.

[53] Dunnette, M.D. & Maetzold, J., "Use of a Weighted Application Blank in Hiring Seasoned Employees," *Journal of Applied Psychology*, 1955, 35, 308-10.

[54] Segal, S.M., Busse, T.V., & Mansfield, R.S., "The Relationship of Scientific Creativity in the Biological Sciences to Predoctoral Accomplishments and Experiences," *American Educational Research Journal*, Winter 1980, 17 (4), 491-502.

[55] Goldsmith, D.B, "The Use of the Personal History Blank as a Salesmanship Test," *Journal of Applied Psychology*, 1922, 6, 149-55.

[56] Eberhardt, B.J. & Muchinsky, P.M., "Biodata Determinants of Vocational Typology: An Integration of Two Paradigms," *Journal of Applied Psychology*, 1982, 67, 714-27:82.

[57] Mount, M.K., Witt, L.A., & Barrick, M.R., "Incremental Validity of Empirically Keyed Biodata Scales Over GMA and the Five Factor Personality Constructs," *Personnel Psychology*, 2000, 53 (2), 299-323.

[58] See West, J. & Karas, M., "Biodata: Meeting Clients' Needs for a Better Way of Recruiting Entry-level Staff," *International Journal of Selection and Assessment*, 1999, 7 (2), 126-31.

[59] See Harold, C.M., McFarland, L.A., & Weekley, J.A., "The Validity of Verifiable and Non-verifiable Biodata Items: An Examination Across Applicants and Incumbents," *International Journal of Selection and Assessment*, 2006, 14 (4), 336-46; Kluger, A.N. & Colella, A., "Beyond the Mean Bias: The Effect of Warning Against Faking on Biodata Item Variances," *Personnel Psychology*, 1993, 46 (4), 763-80; Becker, T.E. & Colquitt, A.L., "Potential Versus Actual Faking of a Biodata Form: An Analysis Along Several Dimensions of Item Type," *Personnel Psychology*, 1992, 45 (2), 389-406.

[60] Stricker, L.J. & Rock, D.A., "Assessing Leadership Potential with a Biographical Measure of Personality Traits," *International Journal of Selection and Assessment*, 1998, 6(3), 164-84.

[61] Mael, F.A., "A Conceptual Rationale for the Domain and Attributes of Biodata Items," *Personnel Psychology*, 1991, 44, 763-927.

[62] Reilly, R.R. & Chao, G.T., "Validity and Fairness of Some Alternative Employee Selection Procedures," *Personnel Psychology*, 1982, 35, 1-62; Schmitt, N., Gooding, R.F., Noe, R.A., & Kirsch, M., "Meta-analyses of Validity Studies Published Between 1964 and 1982 and the Investigation of Study Differences," *Personnel Psychology*, 1984, 37, 407-22; Hunter, J.E. & Hunter, R.F., "Validity and Utility of Alternative Predictors of Job Performance," *Psychological Bulletin*, 1984, 96, 72-98; Snell, A.F., Stokes, G.S., Sands, M.M., & McBride, J.R., "Adolescent Life Experiences as Predictors of Occupational Attainment," *Journal of Applied Psychology*, 1994, 79(1), 131-41.

[63] Phillips, J.M. & Gully, S.M. (2002). "Fairness reactions to personnel selection techniques in Singapore and the United States," International Journal of Human Resource Management, 13, 1186-1205.

[64] Reilly, R.R. & Chao, G.T., "Validity and Fairness of Some Alternative Employee Selection Procedures," *Personnel Psychology*, 1982, 35, 1-62.

[65] Eberhardt, B.J. & Muchinsky, P.M., "Biodata Determinants of Vocational Typology: An Integration of Two Paradigms," *Journal of Applied Psychology*, 1982, 67, 714-27:82.

[66] Pannone, R.D., "Predicting Test Performance: A Content Valid Approach to Screening Applicants," *Personnel Psychology*, 1984, 37, 507-14.

[67] Pannone, R.D., "Blue Collar Selection," In G.S. Stokes, M.D. Mumford, & W.A. Owens (eds.), pp. 261-74. *Biodata Handbook*, 1994. Palo Alto, California: CPP Books.

[68] Wilkinson, L.J., "Generalizable Biodata? An Application to the Vocational Interests of Managers," *Journal of Occupational and Organizational Psychology*, 1997, 70, 49-60.

[69] Hansell, S., "Google Answer to Filling Jobs Is an Algorithm," *New York Times*, January 3, 2007, available online at: http://query.nytimes.com/gst/fullpage.htm l?res=9F06E7DA1730F930A35752C0A9619C8B63&sec=&spon=&pagewante d=1. Accessed February 9, 2009.

[70] Frase-Blunt, M., "Dialing for Candidates," *HR Magazine*, April 2005, pp. 78-82.

[71] Wells, S.J., "Too Good to Hire?" *HR Magazine*, October 2004, pp. 48-54.

[72] Schmidt, F.L., & Hunter, J.E., "Employment Testing: Old Theories and New Research Findings," *American Psychologist*, 1981, 36, 1128-37; Schmidt, F.L. & Hunter, J.E., "The Validity and Utility of Selection Methods in Personnel Psychology: Practical and Theoretical Implications of 85 Years of Research Findings," *Psychological Bulletin*, 1998, 124, 262-74.

[73] Hunter, J.E., "Cognitive Ability, Cognitive Aptitudes, Job Knowledge, and Job Performance," *Journal of Vocational Behavior*, 1986, 29(3), 340-62; Murphy, K., "Is the Relationship Between Cognitive Ability and Job Performance Stable Over Time?," *Human Performance*, 1989, 2, 183-200; Ree, M.J. & Earles, J.A., "Intelligence Is the Best Predictor of Job Performance," *Current Directions in Psychological Science*, 1992, 1, 86-9.

[74] Conlin, M., "Champions of Innovation," *IN*, June 2006, pp. 18-26.

[75] Gully, S.M., Payne, S.C., Koles, K.L.K., "The Impact of Error Training and Individual Differences on Training Outcomes: An Attribute-Treatment Interaction Perspective," *Journal of Applied Psychology*, 2002, 87, pp. 143-55.

[76] Outtz, J.L., "The Role of Cognitive Ability Tests in Employment Selection," *Human Performance*, 2002, 15, 161-71.

[77] Hough, L., Oswald, F.L., Ployhart, R.E., "Determinants, Detection and Amelioration of Adverse Impact in Personnel Selection Procedures: Issues, Evidence and Lessons Learnt," *International Journal of Selection and Assessment*, 2001, 9 (1/2), pp.152-94.

[78] Smither, J.W., Reilly, R.R., Millsap, R.E., Pearlman, K., & Stoffey, R.W., "Applicant Reactions to Selection Procedures," *Personnel Psychology*, 1993, 46, p. 49-76.

[79] Roth, P.L., Bevier, C.A., Bobko, P., Switzer, F.S., & Tyler, P., "Ethnic Group Differences I Cognitive Ability in Employment and Educational Settings: A Meta-analysis," *Personnel Psychology*, 2001, 54 (2), 297–330; Murphy, K.R., "Can Conflicting Perspectives on the Role of g in Personnel Selection be Resolved?" *Human Performance*, 2002, 15, pp. 173-86; Murphy, K.R., Cronin, B.E., & Tam, A.P., "Controversy and Consensus Regarding Use of Cognitive Ability Testing in Organizations," *Journal of Applied Psychology*, 2003, 88, pp. 660-71.

[80] Outtz, J.L., "The Role of Cognitive Ability Tests in Employment Selection," *Human Performance*, 2002, 15, 161-71.

[81] Walker, S., "The NFL's Smartest Team," *The Wall Street Journal Online*, September 30, 2005, available online at: http://online.wsj.com/article_email/ SB112804210724556355-IRjf4NjlaZ4n56rZH2JaqWHm4.html. Accessed February 8, 2009.

[82] *Diaz v. Pan Am World Airways*, 442 F.2d 385 (5th Cir.1971).

[83] Pfeffer, J., "Why Resumes are Just One Piece of the Puzzle," *Business 2.0*, December 1, 2005, available online at: http://money.cnn.com/magazines/ business2/business2_archive/2005/12/01/8364603/index.htm. Accessed June 27, 2006.

[84] Richtel, M., "Online Revolution's Latest Twist: Job Interviews With a Computer," *The New York Times*, February 6, 2000, pp. 1, 21.

85 Canoni, J.D., "Widely Used Psychological Test Found to Violate ADA," *Nixon Peabody LLP Employment Law Alert*, June 16 2005, available online at: http://www.nixonpeabody.com/linked_media/publications/ELA_06162005.pdf#search=%22psychological%20testing%20ada%22. Accessed February 8, 2009.

86 See Ruiz, G., "Staying Out of Legal Hot Water While Conducting Background Checks," *Workforce Management* Online, June 2006, available online at: http://www.workforce.com/section/06/feature/24/39/38/. Accessed February 12, 2009.

87 Guion, R.M. & Gottier, R.F., "Validity of Personality Measures in Personnel Selection," *Personnel Psychology*, 1965, 18, 135–64.; Mischel. W., *Personality and Assessment*, 1968, New York: Wiley; Davis-Blake, A. & Pfeffer, J., "Just a Mirage—The Search for Dispositional Effects in Organizational Research," *Academy of Management Review*, 1989, 14, 385–400.

88 O'Meara, D.P., "Personality Tests Raise Questions of Legality and Effectiveness," *HR Magazine*, January 1994, available online at: http://findarticles.com/p/articles/mi_m3495/is_n1_v39/ai_15162186/pg_1. Accessed February 2, 2009.

89 Mount, M.K. & Barrick, M.R., "The Big Five Personality Dimensions; Implications for Research and Practice in Human Resources Management," in G.R. Ferris (ed.), *Research in Personnel and Human Resources Management*, vol. 13 (Greenwich, CT: JAI Press), pp. 153-200.

90 Vinchur, A.J., Schippmann, J.S., Switzer, F.A., & Roth, P.L., "A Meta-Analysis of the Predictors of Job Performance for Salespeople," *Journal of Applied Psychology*, 1998, 83, 586-97.

91 Barrick, M.R. & Mount, M.K., "The Big Five Personality Dimensions and Job Performance: A Meta-Analysis," *Personnel Psychology*, 1991, 44, 1-26.

92 Vinchur, A.J., Schippmann, J.S., Switzer, F.A., & Roth, P.L., "A Meta-analysis of the Predictors of Job Performance for Salespeople," *Journal of Applied Psychology*, 1998, 83, 586-97; Judge, T.A. & Bono, J.E., "Relationship of Core Self-evaluation Traits—Self-esteem, Generalized Self-efficacy, Locus of control, and Emotional Stability—With Job Satisfaction and Job Performance: A Meta-analysis," *Journal of Applied Psychology*, 2001, 86, 80-92.

93 Mount, M.K., Barrick, M.R., & Stewart, G.L., "Five-Factor Model of Personality and Performance in Jobs Involving Interpersonal Interactions," *Human Performance*, 1998, 11, 145-65.

94 Ibid.

95 Jordan, J. & Cartwright, S., "Selecting Expatriate Managers: Key Traits and Competencies," *Leadership & Organization Development Journal*, April 1998, 19, 89 96.

96 Barrick, M.R. & Mount, M.K., "Yes, Personality Matters: Moving on to More Important Matters," *Human Performance*, 2005, 18 (4), 359-72.

97 Schmidt, F.L., & Hunter, J.E., "The Validity and Utility of Selection Methods in Personnel Psychology: Practical and Theoretical Implications of 85 Years of Research Findings," *Psychological Bulletin*, 1998, 124, 262–74.

[98] Barrick, M.R., Mount, M.K., & Judge, T.A., "The FFM Personality Dimensions and Job Performance: Meta-Analysis of Meta-analyses" [Special issue], *International Journal of Selection and Assessment*, 2001, 9, 9–30.

[99] Ibid.

[100] Mount, M.K., Barrick, M.R., & Stewart, G.L., "Personality Predictors of Performance in Jobs Involving Interaction with Others" [Special issue], *Human Performance*,1998, 11, 145–66.

[101] George, J.M. & Zhou, J., "When Openness to Experience and Conscientiousness are Related to Creative Behavior: An Interactional Approach," *Journal of Applied Psychology*, 2001, 86, 513–24; LePine, J.A., Colquitt, J.A., & Erez, A., "Adaptability to Changing Task Contexts: Effects of General Cognitive Ability, Conscientiousness, and Openness to Experience," *Personnel Psychology*, 2000, 53,563–93.

[102] Barrick, M.R. & Mount, M.K., "Yes, Personality Matters: Moving on to More Important Matters," *Human Performance*, 2005, 18 (4), 359-72.

[103] Costa, P.T. Jr. & McCrae, R.R., "Four Ways Five Factors are Basic," *Personality and Individual Differences*, 1992, 13, 653-65.

[104] Ones, D.S. & Viswesvaran, C., "Bandwidth-fidelity Dilemma in Personality Measurement for Personnel Selection," *Journal of Organizational Behavior*, 1996, 17, 609-26.

[105] Mount, M.K. & Barrick, M.R., "The Big Five Personality Dimensions: Implications for Research and Practice in Human Resources Management," in G.R. Ferris (ed.), *Research in Personnel and Human Resources Management*, 13, Greenwich, CT: JAI Press, pp. 153-200.

[106] Schneider, R.J., Hough, L.M., & Dunnette, M.D., "Broadsided by Broad Traits: How to Sink Science in Five Dimensions or Less," *Journal of Organizational Behavior*, 1996, 17 (6), 639-55.

[107] Frei, R.L. & McDaniel, M.A., "Validity of Customer Service Measures in Personnel Selection: A Review of Criterion and Construct Evidence," *Human Performance*, 1998, 11 (1), 1-27.

[108] Ellingson, J.E., Smith, D.B., & Sackett, P.R., "Investigating the Influence of Social Desirability on Personality Factor Structure," *Journal of Applied Psychology*, 2001, 86, 122-33; Smith, D.B. & Ellingson, J.E., "Substance versus Style: A New Look at Social Desirability in Motivating Contexts," *Journal of Applied Psychology*, 2002, 87, 211-19.

[109] See http://www.unl.edu/buros/.

[110] Rosse, J.G., Miller, J.L., & Ringer, R.C., "The Deterrent Value of Drug and Integrity Testing," *Journal of Business and Psychology*, 1996, 10 (4), 477-85.

[111] See Saroka v. Dayton Hudson, 235 Cal. App. 3d 654 (1991).

[112] See "Another Defeat for MMPI Psychological Test," *FairTest Examiner*, Summer 2000, available online at: http://www.fairtest.org/examarts/Summer%2000/Defeat%20for%20MMPI%20Psych%20Test.html. Accessed May 2, 2008.

[113] Woyke, E., "Attention, Shoplifters," *BusinessWeek* Online, September 11, 2006, available online at: http://www.businessweek.com/magazine/content/06_37/b4000401.htm?chan=tc&campaign_id=bier_tcst0. Accessed February 8, 2009.

[114] See Sackett, P.R. & Wanek, J.E., "New Developments in the Use of Measures of Honesty, Integrity, Conscientiousness, Dependability, Trustworthiness, and Reliability for Personnel Selection," *Personnel Psychology*, 1996, 49, pp. 787-829; Goldberg, J.R., Grenier, R.M., Guion, L.B., Sechrest, LB., & Wing, H., "Questionnaires Used in the Prediction of Trustworthiness in Pre-Employment Selection Decisions: An APA Task Force Report," 1991, Washington, DC: American Psychological Association.

[115] See Ryan, A.M. & Sackett, P.R., "Preemployment Honesty Testing: Fakability, Reactions of Test Takers, and Company Image," *Journal of Business and Psychology*, 1987, 1, 248-56; Cunningham, M.R., Wong, D.T., & Barbee, A.P., "Self-Presentation Dynamics on Overt Integrity Tests: Experimental Studies of the Reid Report," *Journal of Applied Psychology*, 1994, 79, pp. 643-58.

[116] Ones, D.S., Viswesvaran, C., & Schmidt, F.L., "Comprehensive Meta-analysis of Integrity Test Validities: Findings and Implications for Personnel Selection and Theories of Job Performance," *Journal of Applied Psychology*, 1993, 78 (4), 679-703.

[117] Ibid.

[118] Phillips, J.M. & Gully, S.M. (2002). "Fairness reactions to personnel selection techniques in Singapore and the United States," *International Journal of Human Resource Management*, 13, 1186-1205; Steiner, D.D., & Gilliland, S.W. (1996). "Fairness reactions to personnel selection techniques in France and the United States," *Journal of Applied Psychology*, 81, 134-41.

[119] Rosse, J.G., Miller, J.L., & Ringer, R.C., "The Deterrent Value of Drug and Integrity Testing," *Journal of Business and Psychology*, 1996, 10 (4), 477-85.

[120] Arnold, D.W. & Jones, J.W., "Who the Devil's Applying Now?" www.crimchek.com, available online at: http://www.crimcheck.com/employment_testing.htm. Accessed May 3, 2008.

[121] Goldbert, L.R., Grenier, J.R., Guion, R.M., Sechrest, L.B., & Wing, H., "Questionnaires Used in the Prediction of Trustworthiness in Pre-Employment Selection Decisions: An APA Task Force Report," 1991, Washington, DC: American Psychological Association.

[122] Townsend, J.W., "Is Integrity Testing Useful: The Value of Integrity Tests in the Employment Process," *HR Magazine*, July 1992, available online at: http://findarticles.com/p/articles/mi_m3495/is_n7_v37/ai_12787161. Accessed February 12, 2009.

[123] U.S. Department of Labor, "Employee Polygraph Protection Act of 1988 (EPPA)," *Employment Law Guide*, available online at: http://www.dol.gov/compliance/guide/eppa.htm. Accessed February 13, 2009.

[124] Dye, D.M., Reck, M., & McDaniel, M.A., "The Validity of Job Knowledge Measures," *International Journal of Selection and Assessment*, 1993, 1, 153-57.

[125] Steiner, D.D., & Gilliland, S.W., "Fairness Reactions to Personnel Selection Techniques in France and the United States," *Journal of Applied Psychology*, 1996, 81, 134-41; Phillips, J.M. & Gully, S.M., "Fairness Reactions to Personnel Selection Techniques in Singapore and the United States," *International Journal of Human Resource Management*, 2002, 13, 1186-205.

[126] Barber, A.E., Hollenbeck, J.R., Tower, S.L., & Phillips, J.M., "The Effects of Interview Focus on Recruitment Effectiveness: A Field Experiment," 1994, *Journal of Applied Psychology*, 79, 886-96.

[127] Carbonara, P., "Hire for Attitude, Train for Skill," *Fast Company*, August 1996, 4, 73.

[128] Pursell, E.D., Campion, M.A., & Gaylord, S.R., "Structured Interviewing: Avoiding Selection Problems," *Personnel Journal*, 1980, 59(11), pp. 907-12.

[129] Fitzwater, Terry L. *Behavior-based Interviewing: Selecting the Right Person for the Job*, 2000, Menlo Park, CA: Crisp Learning.

[130] "Recruiting, Selecting and Training for Success," tt100.biz, available online at: http://www.thetimes100.co.uk/case_study.php?cID=28&csID=194&pID=1. Accessed July 10, 2008.

[131] Pfeffer, J. "Why Resumes are Just One Piece of the Puzzle," *Business 2.0*, December 1, 2005, available online at: http://money.cnn.com/magazines/business2/business2_archive/2005/12/01/8364603/index.htm. Accessed February 11, 2009.

[132] Taylor, P.J. & Small, B., "Asking Applicants What They Would Do Versus What They Did Do: A Meta-analytic Comparison of Situational and Past Behavior Employment Interview Questions," *Journal of Occupational and Organizational Psychology*, 2002, 75 (3), 277-94.

[133] Freiberg, K. & Freiberg, J., *Nuts! Southwest Airlines' Crazy Recipe for Business and Personal Success*, 1996, Austin: Bard Press.

[134] Kennedy, J., "What To Do When Job Applicants Tell ... Tales of Invented Lives," *Training*, October 1999, 110-14.

[135] "FBI Special Agent Selection Process: Applicant Information Booklet," September 1997, available online at: http://www.fbi.gov/employment/booklet/phase1.htm. Accessed February 11, 2009.

[136] Bianchi, A., "The Character-revealing Handwriting Analysis," *Inc. Magazine*, February 1996, available online at: http://www.inc.com/magazine/19960201/1549.html. Accessed February 11, 2009.

[137] Ben-Shakar, G., Bar-Hillel, M., Blum, Y., Ben-Abba, E., & Flug, A., *Journal of Applied Psychology*, 1986 (71), 645-53.

[138] Phillips, J.M. & Gully, S.M., "Fairness Reactions to Personnel Selection Techniques in Singapore and the United States," *International Journal of Human Resource Management*, 2002, 13, 1186-1205.

[139] See Spohn, J., "The Legal Implications of Graphology," *Washington University Law Quarterly*, Fall 1997, 75 (3), available online at: http://www.wulaw.wustl.edu/WULQ/75-3/753-6.html#fn4. Accessed July 3, 2008.

140 See "The Legal Implications of Graphology," Washington University Law Quarterly, Fall 1997, 75 (3), available online at: http://www.wulaw.wustl.edu/WULQ/75-3/753-6.html#fn4. Accessed July 3, 2008.

141 Zimmerman, E., "Use of Job Simulations Rising Steadily," *Workforce Management* Online, October 10, 2005, available online at: www.workforce.com/section/06/feature/24/18/59. Accessed February 11, 2009.

142 Johne, M. "Prize for Playing the Game: A Career," *Queen's School of Business Media & News*, available online at: http://business.queensu.ca/news/a_career.htm. Accessed August 11, 2008.

143 Ibid.

144 Martinez, M., "Screening for Quality on the Web," *Employment Management Today*, Winter 2004, 9 (1), Available online at: http://www.shrm.org/ema/emt/articles/2004/winter04cover.asp. Accessed February 11, 2009.

145 Johne, M. "Prize for Playing the Game: A Career," *Queen's School of Business Media & News*, available online: http://business.queensu.ca/news/a_career.htm. Accessed August 11, 2008.

146 Carbonara, P., "Hire for Attitude, Train for Skill," *Fast Company*, August 1996, 4, 73.

117 Falcone, P., "Getting Employers to Open Up on a Reference Check," *HR Magazine*, July 1995, available online at: http://findarticles.com/p/articles/mi_m3495/is_n7_v40/ai_17152485. Accessed February 13, 2009.

148 42 U.S.C. § 12112(d)(4) (1994); 29 C.F.R. § 1630.14(c) (2000).

149 42 U.S.C. § 12112(d) (1994); 29 C.F.R. § 1630.14 (1998).

150 American Management Association, AMA 2004 *Workplace Testing Survey: Medical Testing*, 2004, New York, NY: American Management Association, p. 1.

151 American Management Association, *2001 AMA Survey on Workplace Testing: Medical Testing: Summary of Key Findings*, 2001, New York, NY: American Management Association, 1.

152 "US to Outlaw Corporate Prejudice Based on Genes," *New Scientist*, May 5, 2007, available online at: http://www.newscientist.com/channel/life/genetics/mg19426023.300-us-to-outlaw-corporate-prejudice-based-on-genes.html. Accessed March 27, 2009. Also see "The Genetic Information Nondiscrimination Act (GINA) of 2008," available online at http://www.shrm.org/LegalIssues/FederalResources/FederalStatutesRegulationsandGuidanc/Pages/TheGeneticInformationNondiscriminationActof2007.aspx.

153 42 U.S.C. § 12112(d)(3) (1994); 29 C.F.R. § 1630.14(b)(1)-(2) (2000).

154 *Leonel v. American Airlines Inc.*, No. 03-15890 (9th Cir. 2005). See also, Ruiz, G., "Use Care When Conducting Pre-Employment Tests," *Workforce Management* Online, June 2006, available online at: http://www.workforce.com/archive/article/24/41/15.php?ht=care%20when%20conducting%20pre%20employment%20tests%20care%20when%20conducting%20pre%20employment%20tests. Accessed February 10, 2009.

[155] U.S. Department of Labor, "Working Partners News Room," available online at: http://www.dol.gov/asp/programs/drugs/workingpartners/news-room.asp. Accessed February 9, 2009.

[156] U.S. Department of Labor, "Drug Testing," *Elaws — Drug-Free Workplace Advisor*, available online at: http://www.dol.gov/elaws/asp/drugfree/drugs/screen92.asp. Accessed February 9, 2009.

[157] Carr, E., "Current Issues in Employee Substance Abuse Testing," *The Synergist*, May/June 2004, available online at: http://www.dol.gov/asp/programs/drugs/workingpartners/materials/abuse_testing.asp. Accessed January 27, 2009.

[158] McGregor, J., "Background Checks that Never End," *BusinessWeek*, March 20, 2006, 40.

[159] Conlin, M., "You Are What You Post," *BusinessWeek*, March 27, 2006, 52-3.

[160] Frieswick, K., "Background Checks," *CFO Magazine*, August 1, 2005, available online at: http://www.cfo.com/article.cfm/4220232/1/c_4221579?f=insidecfo. Accessed February 1, 2009.

[161] *Fair and Accurate Credit Transactions Act*, Public Law 108-159, 2003, available online at: http://www.ustreas.gov/offices/domestic-finance/financial-institution/cip/pdf/fact-act.pdf. Accessed January 29, 2009.

[162] Ruiz, G., "Staying Out of Legal Hot Water While Conducting Background Checks," *Workforce Management Online*, June 2006, available online at: http://www.workforce.com/section/06/feature/24/39/38/. Accessed January 30, 2009.

[163] Frieswick, K., "Background Checks," *CFO Magazine*, August 1 2005, available online at: http://www.cfo.com/article.cfm/4220232/1/c_4221579?f=insidecfo. Accessed February 1, 2009.

[164] Federal Trade Commission, "Using Consumer Reports: What Employers Need to Know," March 1999, available online at: http://www.ftc.gov/bcp/conline/pubs/buspubs/credempl.shtm. Accessed October 11, 2008.

[165] Ibid.

[166] Crane, A.B., "The ABCs of Pre-Employment Background Checks," *Bankrate.com*, February 16, 2005, available online at: http://www.bankrate.com/brm/news/advice/20050216a1.asp. Accessed February 21, 2009.

[167] *Interim Healthcare of Fort Wayne, Inc. v. Moyer*, 746 N.E.2d 429, 431 (Ind. App. 2001).

[168] Ruiz, G., "Staying Out of Legal Hot Water While Conducting Background Checks," *Workforce Management* Online, June 2006, available online at: http://www.workforce.com/section/06/feature/24/39/38/. Accessed January 30, 2009.

[169] Ibid.

[170] Stevens-Huffman, L., "Hiring Top Sales Performers," *Workforce Management* Online, May 2006, available online at: http://www.workforce.com/archive/feature/24/36/39/index.php?ht=. Accessed June 27, 2006.

[171] Hausknecht, J.P., Day, D.V., & Thomas, S.C., "Applicant Reactions to Selection Procedures: An Updated Model and Meta-Analysis," *Personnel Psychology*, 2004, 57(3), 639-83.

[172] Carbonara, P., "How Nucor Hires: Build Yourself a Job," *Fast Company*, August 1996, 4, 76.

[173] See Potosky, D., Bobko, P., & Roth, P.L., "Forming Composites of Cognitive Ability and Alternative Measures to Predict Job Performance and Reduce Adverse Impact: Corrected Estimates and Realistic Expectations," *International Journal of Selection and Assessment*, 2005, 13 (4), 304-15.

[174] Pfeffer, J. *The Human Equation: Building Profits by Putting People First*, 1998, Boston, MA: Harvard Business School Press.

[175] Freiberg, K. & Freiberg, J., *Nuts! Southwest Airlines' Crazy Recipe for Business and Personal Success*, 1996, Austin: Bard Press.

[176] Pfeffer, J. *The Human Equation: Building Profits by Putting People First*, 1998, Boston, MA: Harvard Business School Press.

[177] Kaihla, P., "Best-kept Secrets of the World's Best Companies," *Business 2.0*, March 23, 2006, available online at http://money.cnn.com/2006/03/23/magazines/business2/business2_bestkeptsecrets/index.htm. Accessed January 16, 2009.

[178] Kaihla, P., "Best-kept Secrets of the World's Best Companies," *Business 2.0*, March 23, 2006, available online at http://money.cnn.com/2006/03/23/magazines/business2/business2_bestkeptsecrets/index.htm, Accessed January 16, 2009; Freiberg, K. & Freiberg, J., *Nuts! Southwest Airlines' Crazy Recipe for Business and Personal Success*, 1996, Austin: Bard Press.

[179] Kaihla, P., "Best-kept Secrets of the World's Best Companies," *Business 2.0*, March 23, 2006, available online at http://money.cnn.com/2006/03/23/magazines/business2/business2_bestkeptsecrets/index.htm. Accessed January 16, 2009; "We Weren't Just Airborne Yesterday," www.southwest.com, available online at: http://www.southwest.com/about_swa/airborne.html, Accessed March 29, 2009.

Index

A

absenteeism 38, 39
adverse action notice 54
adverse employment decision 55
adverse impact 28, 29, 34, 37, 38, 47, 49, 59, 60, 65
agreeableness 35, 36
Allaire Corporation 10
Allaire, J.J. 10
American Express 26
American Psychological Association 39
Americans with Disabilities Act (ADA) 34, 37, 46, 51
Apache Corporation 2
applicant
        characteristics 65
        pool 1, 10
        qualifications 7
assessment(s)
        candidate assessment 1, 41
                external 3, 65
        centers 21, 49
        contingent assessment(s) 19, 50
                methods 20
        effort 10
        external assessment 14, 62
                methods 20, 21
                process 3, 61
                systems 10
        goal 12
        method(s) 3, 12, 13, 14, 17, 20, 26, 33, 36, 39, 57, 59, 61, 63, 65
                evaluative 31
        outcomes 11
        procedures 15
        process 13, 47, 50
        screening assessment methods 19
        system 1, 2, 11, 13, 65
        web-based assessment tools 26
        written assessment tests 47
AT&T 2

B

background check 15, 19, 47, 51, 52, 53, 55, 57
        pre-employment 53

background reports 54
banding 59
behavior(s)
        counterproductive behaviors 38
        employee behavior 26
        job behaviors 16
        work behaviors 37
                observable 16
benchmark responses 43
biodata 21, 28, 29, 30, 31, 33
body of learned information 16
bona fide occupational qualifications (BFOQ) 17, 34
business necessity 28
business strategy 1, 2, 7, 13, 34, 48, 62
        execution 5, 13, 65

C

California Psychological Inventories 35, 37
candidate advancement decisions 27
career opportunities 9
Civil Rights Act 60
Civil Service Commission 15
cognitive ability 36, 38
        tests 15, 20, 21, 31, 32, 33, 38, 59
compassion 7
competencies 3, 7, 14, 61, 65
        core competencies 34
        interpersonal competencies 6
competitive advantage 1, 2, 65
competitiveness 7
complementary fit 10
compliance 3
conscientiousness 35, 36
consumer reporting agency (CRA) 54
contextual performance 59
contractors 16P
        subcontractors 16
cooperativeness 7
cover letter 20, 22
creativity 14
credit checks 15
credit histories 54
culture(s) 1, 2, 7, 33, 44, 57
        cultural differences 28
        organizational culture 8

D

defamation lawsuits 49
Department of Justice 15
Department of Labor 15, 52
disability/disabilities 38, 51
disciplinary problems 39
discrimination 17
disparate impact 33
Doubletree Hotels 40, 41
Drug Free Workplace Act 52
drug screen(s) 19, 57
drug tests 51, 52

E

emotional stability 35, 36
employee attitudes 7
employee characteristic(s) 1, 26
employer image 14, 65
employment test 15
Equal Employment Opportunity Commission
(EEOC) 15, 17
ethical 39
ethics 14, 46
Executive Order 11246 … 16
extraversion 35, 36

F

Facebook 53
Fair and Accurate Credit Transactions Act
(FACTA) 53, 54
Fair Credit Reporting Act (FCRA) 54
fairness 7
faking 37, 38
    faking job proficiency 48
FBI 45
federal regulations 3
Federal Trade Commission (FTC) 53
Fresh Market, The 23

G

Genetic Information Nondiscrimination Act 51
genetic testing 51
genetic tests 15
Google 6, 30, 32, 53
graphology 46
Griggs v. Duke Power Company 15

H

handwriting analysis 46
hiring
    decisions 12, 61
    discrimination 15
    goal(s) 2

manager(s) 12, 13, 17, 23, 26
    interview 64
negligent hiring 49, 55
    defense 53
practices 16
    discrimination in 15
probationary hiring 48
process 20, 39, 62
HR strategy 13
Hunter, Jack 31
hypothetical situations 44

I

innovation strategy 2
innovative 14
integrity 7
    tests 15, 21, 38-9
Interim Healthcare 55
interview(s) 40, 41, 47, 57
    behavioral interviews 41, 42, 43, 45, 47
    recruiter interview 64
    situational interviews 41, 42, 43, 44, 45

J

job analysis 17, 26
job applicant(s) 1, 14, 19, 47
job application(s) 23, 26, 28, 30, 31
    form 24-5, 27
job candidate(s) 1, 2, 3, 5, 12, 14, 19, 23, 47,
    49, 53, 57, 62, 65
    assessing job candidates 5
    assessment 19
    characteristics 3
job knowledge tests 21, 40, 57
job offer, contingent 52, 57
job performance 2, 5, 7, 12, 20, 29, 31, 36,
    37, 61, 63, 64
    past job performance 46
    predicting 19, 38, 59, 65
    predictors of 33
job requirements 7
    relevant 34
job satisfaction 6, 7
job simulations 46-8
    fidelity 46
        tests 47
    motor 46
    verbal 46
job success 2
job tenure 12
job-analysis ratings 61
Johnson & Johnson (J&J) 8, 34

K

Kaufman Brief Intelligence Test 32
Kroger 26

L

Larsen, Ralph 8
legal
    compliance 15, 17, 51
    counsel 3
    issues 15
    requirements 65
L'Oréal 47, 48

M

McDonald's 13, 23, 44
medical tests 51, 52
Men's Wearhouse 6
Mental Measurements Yearbook 37
Microsoft 2
Minnesota Multiphasic Personality Inventory
    (MMPI) 34-5, 37
MyBackgroundCheck.com 54
    MyJobHistory.com 54
MySpace 53

N

noncognitive
    ability tests 33-4
    skills 45
Nucor Steel 57

O

online applications 26
openness to experience 35, 36
organizational commitment 6, 7
organizational expectations and standards 8
organizational outcomes 7

P

Pace, Dave 8
peer performance reviews 30
performance 1, 8, 10, 12, 36
    improvements 12
personal characteristics 28
personality
    assessment(s) 34-8, 37, 38, 57
    inventories 33
    testing 21
    tests 36, 37, 38
    traits 35
person-group fit (also person-team fit) 6, 9
person-job fit 5, 7, 9
person-organization fit 7, 9
person-vocation fit 8, 9
physical abilities 33
Polygraph Protection Act 39
polygraph tests 39-40
preliminary qualifications 31

Principles for the Validation and Use of Personnel Selection Procedures, The 16
privacy 14, 28, 37, 46, 51, 52, 54
    needs 15
    rights 39
productivity 1
promotability 2
promotions 29
Prudential Realty 47
psychomotor 33

R

race norming 60
racial differences 33
Raven's Progressive Matrices 32
reasonably related 15
recruiters 12, 17, 26
recruiting 8, 40
recruitment
    process 47
    profile 14
    targeted recruitment 59
reference checks 21, 47, 49, 50, 57
Renda Broadcasting 57
resume(s) 20, 22, 23, 63
    screen 57
retention 7, 8, 14
return on investment 11, 12, 65

S

Schmidt, Frank 31
screening
    applicants 26
    criteria 14
    preliminary screening questions 26
selection process 14
sensory 33
shareholder reactions 65
Sherwin-Williams 26
Silicon Graphics 3
simulation(s) 21, 57
    performance 64
situational judgment tests 21, 45
skills assessment 57
Southwest Airlines 44, 49, 57, 62, 63
staffing
    effort 5
    function 1
    goals 5
    outcome(s) 5, 6
    process 12
    strategic staffing 13
stakeholders 12
Standards for Educational and Psychological Testing 16
Starbucks 8
stereotypes 17
structured interviews 21, 41, 42, 45
    steps in 42
supplementary fit 10

T
talent 10
    philosophy 1
targeted applicant characteristics 61
teammates 6
technology 20
telephone screens 31
tenure 29
theft 39
Tiffany's 2
Title VII of the Civil Rights Act 15
training effectiveness 14
training time 14

U
Uniform Guidelines on Employment Selection
    Procedures (UGESP) 15, 16

V
valued employees 9
values
    assessment 37
    core values 8
    key values 34
    organizational values 7
Vault.com 44
Verified Person 53

W
Wal-Mart 1
Wechsler Abbreviated Scale of Intelligence
    32
weighted application blank(s) 26, 27, 30, 31
weighted application forms 21
WetFeet.com 44
Wonderlic Personnel Test 32
work ethic 7
work processes 7
work sample(s) 21, 48-9
    trainability tests 48
worker adjustment 8
workgroup 6, 10

Y
Yahoo! 2

Z
Zimmer, George 6

Acknowledgments

We would like to thank our sons, Ryan and Tyler, for their support and patience while we wrote this book. We would also like to thank Pearson for allowing us to adapt some of the material from our book, Strategic Staffing, for use in this series. We also thank the reviewers—especially Laura Ostroff, director of Total Rewards and HRIS, Bon Secours Health System, Inc.—and the SHRM staff for this opportunity and for their suggestions and insights. If you have feedback about this book or if you would like to contact us for any reason, please e-mail us at phillipsgully@gmail.com.

About the Authors

Jean M. Phillips, Ph.D., is an associate professor of human resource management at the *School of Management and Labor Relations, Rutgers University.* Dr. Phillips is a current or former member of several editorial boards, including *Personnel Psychology, Journal of Applied Psychology, and Journal of Management.* She received the 2004 Cummings Scholar Award from the Organizational Behavior Division of the Academy of Management and was among the top five percent of published authors in two of the top human resource management journals during the 1990s. She is also the co-author of the college textbooks *Managing Now!* (2007) and *Strategic Staffing* (2008), and consults in the areas of recruiting and staffing, linking employee surveys to organizational outcomes, and team effectiveness. She can be reached at phillipsgully@gmail.com.

Stanley M. Gully, Ph.D., is an associate professor of human resource management at the School of Management and Labor Relations, Rutgers University. He is a current or former member of the editorial boards of *Academy of Management Journal, Journal of Applied Psychology, Journal of Organizational Behavior,* and *Journal of Management.* He received multiple awards for his teaching, research, and service, including a research award from the American Society for Training & Development. His paper on general self-efficacy is in the top 10 most read papers in *Organizational Research Methods* and his meta-analysis on cohesion is in the top three most cited papers in *Small Group Research.* He is the co-author of *Strategic Staffing* (2008) and consults in the areas of recruiting and staffing, employee engagement, team effectiveness, and organizational learning interventions. He can be reached at phillipsgully@gmail.com.

Additional SHRM-Published Books

The Cultural Fit Factor: Creating an Employment Brand that Attracts, Retains, and Repels the Right Employees
By Lizz Pellet

The Employer's Immigration Compliance Desk Reference
By Gregory H. Siskind

Employment Termination Source Book
By Wendy Bliss and Gene Thornton

The Essential Guide to Workplace Investigations: How to Handle Employee Complaints & Problems
By Lisa Guerin

Hiring Source Book
By Catherine D. Fyock

Hiring Success: The Art and Science of Staffing Assessment and Employee Selection
By Steven Hunt

Human Resource Essentials: Your Guide to Starting and Running the HR Function
By Lin Grensing-Pophal

Leading With Your Heart: Diversity and Ganas for Inspired Inclusion
By Cari M. Dominguez and Jude A. Sotherlund

Outsourcing Human Resources Functions: How, Why, When, and When Not to Contract for HR Services, 2d ed.
By Mary F. Cook and Scott B. Gildner

Smart Policies for Workplace Technologies: E-mail, Blogs, Cell Phones and More
By Lisa Guerin

Stop Bullying at Work: Strategies and Tools for HR and Legal Professionals
By Teresa A. Daniel

Strategic Staffing: A Comprehensive System for Effective Workforce Planning, 2nd ed.
By Thomas P. Bechet

For these and other SHRM-published books, please visit www.shrm.org/publications/books/pages/default.aspx.